150 Recipes

150 BAKING *recipes*

INSPIRED IDEAS FOR EVERYDAY COOKING

150 CAKE *recipes*

CHICKEN *recipes*

INSPIRED IDEAS FOR EVERYDAY COOKING

150 CUPCAKE & MUFFIN *recipes*

INSPIRED IDEAS FOR EVERYDAY COOKING

150 FAST & SIMPLE *recipes*

INSPIRED IDEAS FOR EVERYDAY COOKING

150 INDIAN *recipes*

INSPIRED IDEAS FOR EVERYDAY COOKING

150 PASTA *recipes*

INSPIRED IDEAS FOR EVERYDAY COOKING

150 SLOW COOKER *recipes*

INSPIRED IDEAS FOR EVERYDAY COOKING

150 STIR-FRY *recipes*

INSPIRED IDEAS FOR EVERYDAY COOKING

150 STUDENT *recipes*

INSPIRED IDEAS FOR EVERYDAY COOKING

150 TAPAS *recipes*

INSPIRED IDEAS FOR EVERYDAY COOKING

150 VEGETARIAN *recipes*

INSPIRED IDEAS FOR EVERYDAY COOKING

D0586448

150

BAKING
recipes

....

INSPIRED IDEAS FOR
EVERYDAY COOKING

CONTENTS

INTRODUCTION

Baking has always been popular and the best news for all budding home bakers out there is that it has become even more so in recent years – baking mania is back! Baking is hugely enjoyable, relaxing and satisfying (not forgetting, delicious to eat too!) and the variety of delicious goodies you can create at home is considerable. Baking can also be therapeutic, as it can take your mind off more immediate everyday concerns and allows you to focus on something positive and fulfilling, with very tasty results indeed!

Baking is enormous fun and it brings people together, thus creating the perfect opportunity to share and enjoy a bounty of home-baked delights. So, be inspired, get set for a blitz on baking and then enjoy munching your

way through some sensational cakes, bakes, bars, breads, tarts and pies. We feature a magnificent medley of brilliant bakes, from a selection of easy small bakes and bars to some more elaborate and impressive cakes and desserts.

We begin this baking bonanza with some marvellous cupcakes and muffins, including temptations such as Hummingbird Cupcakes, Apple Streusel Cupcakes, Triple Chocolate Chip Muffins and Blueberry Muffins.

Next up is an enticing selection of small bites, cookies and bars, ideal for sharing, so why not indulge your family and friends with delights such as rich Chocolate Cheesecake Brownies, melt-in-the-mouth Peanut Butter Cookies or appetizing Apricot Flapjacks? To satisfy younger appetites, the brilliantly named Snickerdoodle Whoopie Pies or yummy Marshmallow S'mores and Rocky Road Bars are sure to satisfy their sweet cravings.

Impress your friends with one of our fabulous cakes, from homely favourites such as Chocolate Fudge Cake, Lemon Drizzle Loaf and Rich Fruit Cake, to more impressive creations such as Citrus Mousse Cake and Pineapple and Coconut Ring Cake.

Let yourself be tempted by our collection of delectable desserts. We include ever-popular classics such as Rhubarb Crumble and Chocolate Fondant Pudding, plus numerous other sumptuous sensations including Meringue Torte, Cappuccino Soufflés and Summer Fruit Tartlets.

Our final section of this superb baking feast features a tempting assortment of sweet and savoury breads and sweet pies. It's hard to beat the enticing aromas and flavours of freshly baked loaves, so it is little wonder that baking bread is one of life's real and satisfying pleasures. Try your hand at creating breads from all over the world, including Sourdough Bread, Bagels and Seeded Rye Bread, then let yourself be tempted by some truly scrumptious sweet pies, including Banoffee Pie and Lemon Meringue Pie.

You don't need a lot of specialist equipment for baking and you will probably already have most things you need. Good quality baking tins in a variety of shapes and sizes are a worthwhile purchase, as are a reliable set of kitchen scales and a good set of mixing bowls. Spatulas and wooden spoons are useful and a hand-held whisk or electric stand mixer will prove invaluable when making cake mixtures or kneading dough. If you are new to baking, make some of the quick and easy recipes first, before then trying some of the more elaborate ones – you'll be amazed at how easy it is to create beautiful bakes! Always make sure you weigh out all your ingredients carefully and have them prepared before you begin a recipe, and don't forget to preheat the oven before you start, or when specified in the recipe.

Home-baked goodies make wonderful gifts too, and there's nothing more satisfying than the delight on someone's face when you give them a homemade edible gift. Bakes can be wrapped simply in cellophane bags and tied with pretty ribbon or raffia, or you can arrange them in attractive gift boxes or baskets to create an impressive present.

CUPCAKES & MUFFINS

CLASSIC VANILLA CUPCAKES

Makes: 12

Prep: 25 mins,
plus cooling

Cook: 15–20 mins

Ingredients

175 g/6 oz unsalted butter,
softened

175 g/6 oz caster sugar

3 large eggs, beaten

1 tsp vanilla extract

175 g/6 oz self-raising flour

Frosting

150 g/5½ oz unsalted butter,
softened

3 tbsp double cream or milk

1 tsp vanilla extract

300 g/10½ oz icing sugar,
sifted

hundreds and thousands,
to decorate

Method

1 Preheat the oven to 180°C/350°F/Gas Mark 4.
Place 12 paper cases in a cupcake tin.

2 Put the butter and caster sugar into a bowl and
beat together until pale and creamy. Gradually
beat in the eggs and vanilla extract. Sift in the
flour and fold in gently.

3 Divide the mixture evenly between the paper
cases and bake in the preheated oven for
15–20 minutes, or until risen and firm to the touch.
Transfer to a wire rack and leave to cool.

4 To make the frosting, put the butter into a bowl
and beat with an electric mixer for 2–3 minutes,
or until pale and creamy. Beat in the cream and
vanilla extract. Gradually beat in the icing sugar
and continue beating until the buttercream is
light and fluffy.

5 Use a palette knife to swirl the frosting over the
tops of the cupcakes. Decorate with hundreds
and thousands.

★ Variation

To make bite-size cupcakes for children's parties,
divide the batter among 30 mini cupcake
paper cases and reduce the cooking time to
8–10 minutes.

FAIRY CUPCAKES

Makes: 16

Prep: 25 mins,
plus cooling

Cook: 15–20 mins

Ingredients

115 g/4 oz unsalted butter

115 g/4 oz caster sugar

2 eggs, beaten

115 g/4 oz self-raising flour

sugar flowers, hundreds and
thousands, glacé cherries
and/or chocolate strands,
to decorate

Icing

200 g/7 oz icing sugar

about 2 tbsp lukewarm
water

few drops of food colouring
(optional)

Method

1 Preheat the oven to 180°C/350°F/Gas Mark 4. Put
16 double-layer paper cases on a baking sheet.

2 Place the butter and caster sugar in a large
bowl and cream together until pale and fluffy.
Gradually add the eggs, beating well after each
addition. Fold in the flour, using a metal spoon.

3 Spoon the mixture into the paper cases and
bake in the preheated oven for 15–20 minutes,
until well risen. Remove from the oven and place
on a wire rack to cool.

4 For the icing, sift the icing sugar into a bowl and
add enough water to mix to a smooth paste,
thick enough to coat the back of a spoon. Stir
in a few drops of food colouring, if using, then
spread over the cakes.

5 Decorate the cupcakes with sugar flowers,
hundreds and thousands and glacé cherries,
and serve.

FUNFETTI CUPCAKES

Makes: 12   **Prep: 35 mins,**   **Cook: 25 mins**
plus cooling

Ingredients

190 g/6¾ oz plain flour

1½ tsp baking powder

¼ tsp salt

55 g/2 oz unsalted butter, softened

55 g/2 oz vegetable shortening

125 g/4½ oz caster sugar

2 tsp vanilla extract

4 large egg whites

125 ml/4 fl oz milk

75 g/2¾ oz hundreds and thousands

Frosting

2 large egg whites

100 g/3½ oz granulated sugar

160 g/5¾ oz unsalted butter, softened

2 tsp vanilla extract

Method

1 Preheat the oven to 180°C/350°F/Gas Mark 4 and line a 12-hole cupcake tin with paper cases.

2 Sift together the flour, baking powder and salt in a bowl. Put the butter, shortening and caster sugar into a separate bowl and beat until pale and fluffy. Add the vanilla extract, then add the egg whites, one at a time, beating between each addition. Add half of the flour mixture and the milk and beat until incorporated. Add the remaining flour mixture and mix. Stir in two thirds of the hundreds and thousands.

3 Spoon the batter into the paper cases and bake for 20 minutes, until risen and golden. Leave to cool in the tin for 1–2 minutes, then transfer to a wire rack to cool.

4 To make the frosting, put the egg whites and granulated sugar in a heatproof bowl set over a saucepan of gently simmering water and whisk until the sugar has dissolved. Remove from the heat and whisk for 4–5 minutes. Add the butter, 2 tablespoons at a time, and continue to whisk until it holds stiff peaks. Add the vanilla extract and beat until just combined. Spoon the frosting into a piping bag fitted with a star-shaped tip. Pipe the frosting onto the cupcakes and sprinkle with the remaining hundreds and thousands.

CHOCOLATE BUTTERFLY CUPCAKES

Makes: 12

Prep: 30 mins,
plus cooling

Cook: 15 mins

Ingredients

125 g/4½ oz soft tub margarine

125 g/4½ oz caster sugar

150 g/5½ oz self-raising flour, sifted

2 large eggs

2 tbsp cocoa powder, sifted

25 g/1 oz plain chocolate, melted

icing sugar, sifted, for dusting

Frosting

85 g/3 oz butter, softened

175 g/6 oz icing sugar

25 g/1 oz plain chocolate, melted

Method

1 Preheat the oven to 180°C/350°F/Gas Mark 4. Put 12 paper baking cases in a bun tray, or put 12 double-layer paper cases on a baking tray.

2 Put the margarine, sugar, flour, eggs and cocoa powder in a large bowl and, using an electric hand whisk, beat together until just smooth. Beat in the melted chocolate. Spoon the mixture into the paper cases, filling them three-quarters full.

3 Bake the cupcakes in the preheated oven for 15 minutes, or until springy to the touch. Transfer to a wire rack and leave to cool.

4 To make the frosting, put the butter in a bowl and beat until fluffy. Sift in the icing sugar and beat together until smooth. Add the melted chocolate and beat together until well mixed.

5 When the cupcakes are cold, use a serrated knife to cut a circle from the top of each cake and then cut each circle in half. Spread or pipe a little of the frosting onto the centre of each cupcake and press 2 semi-circular halves into it at an angle to resemble butterfly wings. Dust with sifted icing sugar before serving.

CHOCOLATE CHIP COOKIE CUPCAKES

Makes: 12

Prep: 35 mins,
plus cooling

Cook: 30–35 mins

Ingredients

250 g/9 oz uncooked ready-made chocolate chip cookie dough

190 g/6¾ oz plain flour

1½ tsp baking powder

¼ tsp salt

115 g/4 oz unsalted butter, softened

50 g/1¾ oz caster sugar

100 g/3½ oz soft light brown sugar

2 tsp vanilla extract

2 large eggs

125 ml/4 fl oz milk

50 g/1¾ oz plain chocolate chips, to decorate

Frosting

3 large egg whites

160 g/5¾ oz soft light brown sugar

160 g/5¾ oz unsalted butter, softened

1½ tsp vanilla extract

Method

1 Preheat the oven to 190°C/375°F/Gas Mark 5 and line a 12-hole cupcake tin with paper cases.

2 Drop rounded spoonfuls of cookie dough into the paper cases and bake in the preheated oven for 8–10 minutes, or until the cookies have begun to brown. Remove from the oven and reduce the oven temperature to 180°C/350°F/Gas Mark 4.

3 Sift together the flour, baking powder and salt in a bowl. Put the butter, caster sugar and brown sugar into a separate bowl and beat until pale and fluffy. Add the vanilla extract, then add the eggs, one at a time, beating after each addition. Add half of the flour mixture and the milk and beat until incorporated. Add the remaining flour mixture and mix.

4 Spoon the batter on top of the cookie bases and bake for 20 minutes, until risen and a cocktail stick inserted into the centre of a cupcake comes out clean. Leave to cool in the tin for 1–2 minutes, then transfer to a wire rack to cool completely.

5 To make the frosting, put the egg whites and brown sugar in a heatproof bowl set over a saucepan of gently simmering water and whisk until the sugar is completely dissolved. Remove

from the heat and whisk the mixture for 4–5 minutes. Add the butter, 2 tablespoons at a time, and continue to beat until it holds stiff peaks. Add the vanilla extract and beat until just combined. Spoon the frosting into a piping bag fitted with a star-shaped tip and pipe onto the cupcakes, then sprinkle with chocolate chips.

ULTIMATE CHOCOLATE CUPCAKES

Makes: 14

Prep: 25 mins,
plus cooling & chilling

Cook: 20–25 mins

Ingredients

115 g/4 oz self-raising flour

½ tsp baking powder

1½ tbsp cocoa powder

115 g/4 oz butter, softened

115 g/4 oz caster sugar

2 large eggs, beaten

55 g/2 oz plain chocolate, melted

Frosting

150 g/5½ oz plain chocolate, finely chopped

200 ml/7 fl oz double cream

140 g/5 oz unsalted butter, softened

280 g/10 oz icing sugar

chocolate shapes and gold dragées, to decorate (optional)

Method

1 Preheat the oven to 180°C/350°F/Gas Mark 4. Place 14 paper cases in a bun tin.

2 Sift the flour, baking powder and cocoa powder into a large bowl. Add the butter, caster sugar and eggs and beat together until smooth. Fold in the melted chocolate.

3 Divide the mixture evenly between the paper cases. Bake in the preheated oven for 15–20 minutes, or until risen and firm to the touch. Transfer to a wire rack and leave to cool.

4 To make the frosting, put the chocolate in a heatproof bowl. Heat the cream in a saucepan until boiling, then pour over the chocolate and stir until smooth. Leave to cool for 20 minutes, stirring occasionally, until thickened. Put the butter in a bowl, sift in the icing sugar and beat until smooth. Beat in the chocolate mixture. Chill for 15–20 minutes.

5 Spoon the frosting into a piping bag fitted with a large star nozzle. Pipe swirls of frosting on top of each cupcake. Decorate with chocolate shapes and gold dragées, if using.

CUPCAKES & MUFFINS

MOLTEN-CENTRED CHOCOLATE CUPCAKES

Makes: 8   **Prep: 20 mins**   **Cook: 20 mins**

Ingredients

g/2 oz soft tub margarine

55 g/2 oz caster sugar

1 large egg

85 g/3 oz self-raising flour, sifted

osp cocoa powder, sifted

55 g/2 oz plain chocolate

icing sugar, sifted, for dusting

Method

1 Preheat the oven to 190°C/375°F/Gas Mark 5. Put 8 paper baking cases in a bun tray, or put 8 double-layer paper cases on a baking tray.

2 Put the margarine, sugar, egg, flour and cocoa powder in a large bowl and, using an electric hand whisk, beat together until just smooth.

3 Spoon half of the mixture into the paper cases. Using a teaspoon, make an indentation in the centre of each cake. Break the chocolate evenly into 8 squares and place a piece in each indentation, then spoon the remaining cake mixture on top.

4 Bake the cupcakes in the preheated oven for 20 minutes, or until well risen and springy to the touch. Leave the cupcakes for 2–3 minutes before serving warm, dusted with sifted icing sugar.

CUPCAKES & MUFFINS

RED VELVET CUPCAKES

Makes: 12

Prep: 25 mins,
plus cooling

Cook: 15–20 mins

Ingredients

140 g/5 oz plain flour

1 tsp bicarbonate of soda

2 tbsp cocoa powder

115 g/4 oz butter, softened

140 g/5 oz caster sugar

1 large egg, beaten

125 ml/4 fl oz buttermilk

1 tsp vanilla extract

1 tbsp red food colouring

red coloured sugar or red
sugar sprinkles, to decorate

Frosting

140 g/5 oz full-fat
soft cheese

85 g/3 oz unsalted butter,
softened

280 g/10 oz icing sugar,
sifted

Method

1 Preheat the oven to 180°C/350°F/Gas Mark 4.
Place 12 paper cases in a bun tin.

2 Sift together the flour, bicarbonate of soda and
cocoa powder. Place the butter and caster
sugar in a separate bowl and beat together unti
pale and creamy. Gradually beat in the egg
and half the flour mixture. Beat in the buttermilk,
vanilla extract and food colouring. Fold in the
remaining flour mixture. Divide the mixture evenly
between the paper cases.

3 Bake the cupcakes in the preheated oven for
15–20 minutes, or until risen and firm to the touch
Transfer to a wire rack and leave to cool.

4 To make the frosting, put the soft cheese and
butter in a bowl and blend together with a
spatula. Beat in the icing sugar until smooth
and creamy. Swirl the frosting on the top of the
cupcakes. Sprinkle with the red sugar.

HUMMINGBIRD CUPCAKES

Makes: 12

Prep: 30 mins, plus cooling

Cook: 15–20 mins

Ingredients

150 g/5½ oz plain flour

¾ tsp bicarbonate of soda

1 tsp ground cinnamon

125 g/4½ oz soft light brown sugar

2 eggs, beaten

100 ml/3½ fl oz sunflower oil

1 ripe banana (about 85 g/3 oz peeled weight), mashed

2 canned pineapple rings, drained and finely chopped

25 g/1 oz pecan nuts, finely chopped, plus extra sliced pecan nuts to decorate

Frosting

140 g/5 oz full-fat soft cheese

70 g/2½ oz unsalted butter, softened

1 tsp vanilla extract

280 g/10 oz icing sugar, sifted

Method

1 Preheat the oven to 180°C/350°F/Gas Mark 4. Place 12 paper cases in a bun tin.

2 Sift the flour, bicarbonate of soda and cinnamon into a bowl and stir in the sugar. Add the eggs, oil, banana, pineapple and chopped pecan nuts and mix thoroughly. Divide the mixture evenly between the paper cases.

3 Bake the cupcakes in the preheated oven for 15–20 minutes, or until risen, golden and firm to the touch. Transfer to a wire rack and leave to cool.

4 To make the frosting, put the soft cheese, butter and vanilla extract in a bowl and blend together with a spatula. Beat in the icing sugar until smooth and creamy. Pipe or swirl the frosting on the top of the cupcakes. Decorate with sliced pecan nuts.

VANILLA CHAI TEA CUPCAKES

Makes: 12

Prep: 30 mins,
plus steeping & cooling

Cook: 30 mins

Ingredients

125 ml/4 fl oz milk

3 chai tea bags

190 g/6¾ oz plain flour

1½ tsp baking powder

¼ tsp each ground cinnamon, ground ginger, ground nutmeg and ground allspice, mixed

¼ tsp salt

115 g/4 oz unsalted butter, softened

200 g/7 oz caster sugar

1 tsp vanilla extract

2 large eggs

1 tsp ground cinnamon and 1 tbsp granulated sugar, mixed, to decorate

Frosting

3 large egg whites

150 g/5½ oz granulated sugar

225 g/8 oz unsalted butter, softened

1 tsp vanilla extract

1 tsp ground cinnamon

Method

1 Preheat the oven to 180°C/350°F/Gas Mark 4 and line a 12-hole cupcake tin with paper cases.

2 Heat the milk in a small saucepan until just boiling. Add the tea bags, remove from the heat and leave to steep for 15 minutes. Remove and discard the tea bags and set the milk aside to cool completely.

3 Sift together the flour, baking powder, mixed spices and salt in a bowl. Put the butter and caster sugar into a separate bowl and beat until pale and fluffy. Add the vanilla extract, then add the eggs, one at a time, beating after each addition, until combined. Add half of the flour mixture and the tea-infused milk and beat until combined. Add the remaining flour and mix.

4 Spoon the batter into the prepared paper cases and bake in the preheated oven for 20 minutes, until risen and golden. Leave to cool in the tin for 1–2 minutes, then transfer to a wire rack to cool completely.

5 To make the frosting, put the egg whites and granulated sugar in a heatproof bowl set over a saucepan of gently simmering water and whisk until the sugar has completely dissolved. Remove from the heat and whisk the mixture for 4–5 minutes. Add the butter, 2 tablespoons at a

time, and continue to beat until it holds stiff peaks. Add the vanilla extract and cinnamon and beat until just combined. Spoon the frosting into a piping bag fitted with a star-shaped tip and pipe onto the cupcakes.

6 To decorate, sprinkle the cinnamon-sugar over the top of the cupcakes.

APPLE STREUSEL CUPCAKES

Makes: 14

Prep: 25 mins,
plus cooling

Cook: 20 mins

Ingredients

½ tsp bicarbonate of soda

280 g/10 oz apple sauce (from a jar)

55 g/2 oz butter, softened, or soft margarine

85 g/3 oz demerara sugar

1 large egg, beaten

175 g/6 oz self-raising flour

½ tsp ground cinnamon

½ tsp freshly grated nutmeg

Topping

50 g/1¾ oz plain flour

50 g/1¾ oz demerara sugar

¼ tsp ground cinnamon

¼ tsp freshly grated nutmeg

35 g/1¼ oz butter, softened

Method

1 Preheat the oven to 180°C/350°F/Gas Mark 4. Place 14 paper cases in a bun tin.

2 To make the topping, put the flour, demerara sugar, cinnamon and nutmeg in a bowl. Cut the butter into small pieces, then add to the bowl and rub it in with your fingertips until the mixture resembles fine breadcrumbs.

3 Add the bicarbonate of soda to the apple sauce and stir until dissolved. Place the butter and demerara sugar in a large bowl and beat together until pale and creamy. Gradually beat in the egg. Sift in the flour, cinnamon and nutmeg and, using a metal spoon, fold into the mixture, alternating with the apple sauce mixture.

4 Divide the mixture evenly between the paper cases. Scatter the topping over the cupcakes and press down gently. Bake in the preheated oven for 20 minutes, or until risen, golden and firm to the touch. Transfer to a wire rack and leave to cool.

BLACKBERRY CRUMBLE CUPCAKES

Makes: 6 **Prep: 20 mins** **Cook: 25–30 mins**

Ingredients

115 g/4 oz butter, softened, plus extra for greasing

115 g/4 oz self-raising flour

½ tsp baking powder

115 g/4 oz caster sugar

2 eggs

175 g/6 oz blackberries

whipped cream or custard, to serve

Crumble topping

85 g/3 oz self-raising flour

55 g/2 oz demerara sugar

55 g/2 oz butter, chilled and diced

Method

1. Preheat the oven to 190°C/375°F/Gas Mark 5. Grease six 200-ml/7-fl oz ovenproof teacups or dishes (such as ramekins) with butter.

2. To make the topping, mix the flour and sugar in a bowl. Add the butter and rub in until the mixture resembles coarse breadcrumbs.

3. To make the sponge, sift the flour and baking powder into a bowl. Add the butter, caster sugar and eggs and, using an electric hand whisk, beat together until smooth. Spoon the mixture into the cups or dishes and level the surface. Top with the blackberries. Spoon the crumble topping over the blackberries.

4. Put the cups or dishes on a baking sheet and bake in the preheated oven for 25–30 minutes until the crumble topping is golden brown. Serve warm with whipped cream.

CUPCAKES & MUFFINS

PURE INDULGENCE ALMOND CUPCAKES

Makes: 12

Prep: 25 mins, plus cooling

Cook: 25 mins

Ingredients

100 g/3½ oz butter, softened, or soft margarine

100 g/3½ oz caster sugar

2 eggs, lightly beaten

¼ tsp almond extract

4 tbsp single cream

175 g/6 oz plain flour

1½ tsp baking powder

70 g/2½ oz ground almonds

toasted flaked almonds, to decorate

Buttercream

115 g/4 oz unsalted butter, softened

225 g/8 oz icing sugar

a few drops of almond extract

Method

1 Preheat the oven to 180°C/350°F/Gas Mark 4. Put 12 paper cases in a cupcake tray.

2 Place the butter and caster sugar in a large bowl and beat together until light and fluffy. Gradually beat in the eggs, then add the almond extract and cream. Sift in the flour and baking powder and, using a metal spoon, fold into the mixture with the ground almonds.

3 Spoon the mixture into the paper cases. Bake in the preheated oven for 25 minutes, or until risen, golden and firm to the touch. Transfer to a wire rack and leave to cool.

4 To make the buttercream, place the butter in a large bowl and beat until creamy. Sift in the icing sugar, add the almond extract and beat together until smooth. Spread the buttercream over the cupcakes and decorate with flaked almonds.

CUPCAKES & MUFFINS

RASPBERRY ALMOND CUPCAKES

Makes: 14

Prep: 15 mins,
plus cooling

Cook: 25–30 mins

Ingredients

115 g/4 oz butter, softened
85 g/3 oz caster sugar
½ tsp almond extract
2 eggs, lightly beaten
85 g/3 oz self-raising flour
55 g/2 oz ground almonds
85 g/3 oz fresh raspberries
2 tbsp flaked almonds
icing sugar, for dusting

Method

1 Preheat the oven to 180°C/350°F/Gas Mark 4.
Put 14 paper cases in 2 bun trays or put
14 double-layer paper cases on a baking tray.

2 Put the butter, sugar and almond extract in a
bowl and beat together until light and fluffy.
Gradually beat in the eggs. Sift in the flour
and, using a metal spoon, fold into the mixture
with the ground almonds. Gently fold in the
raspberries. Spoon the mixture into the paper
cases. Scatter the flaked almonds over the top.

3 Bake the cupcakes in the preheated oven for
25–30 minutes or until golden brown and firm to
the touch. Transfer to a wire rack and leave to
cool. Dust with sifted icing sugar.

CUPCAKES & MUFFINS

SHREDDED ORANGE CUPCAKES

Makes: 12

Prep: 20 mins, plus cooling

Cook: 20–25 mins

Ingredients

85 g/3 oz butter, softened

85 g/3 oz caster sugar

1 large egg, lightly beaten

85 g/3 oz self-raising flour, sifted

25 g/1 oz ground almonds

grated rind and juice of 1 small orange

Orange topping

grated rind and juice of 1 small orange

55 g/2 oz caster sugar

15 g/½ oz toasted flaked almonds

Method

1 Preheat the oven to 180°C/350°F/Gas Mark 4. Put 12 paper cases in a bun tray, or put 12 double-layer paper cases on a baking tray.

2 Put the butter and sugar in a bowl and beat together until light and fluffy. Gradually beat in the egg. Add the flour, ground almonds and orange rind and, using a large metal spoon, fold into the mixture. Fold in the orange juice. Spoon the mixture into the paper cases.

3 Bake the cupcakes in the preheated oven for 20–25 minutes, or until well risen and golden brown.

4 Meanwhile, make the topping. Put the orange rind, orange juice and sugar in a saucepan and heat gently, stirring, until the sugar has dissolved, then simmer for 5 minutes.

5 When the cupcakes have cooked, prick them all over with a skewer. Spoon the warm syrup and rind over each cupcake, then scatter the flaked almonds on top. Transfer to a wire rack and leave to cool.

CUPCAKES & MUFFINS

RASPBERRY DAIQUIRI CUPCAKES

Makes: 12

Prep: 35 mins,
plus cooling & chilling

Cook: 30 mins

Ingredients

190 g/6¾ oz plain flour

1½ tsp baking powder

¼ tsp salt

115 g/4 oz unsalted butter, softened

200 g/7 oz caster sugar

2 large eggs

125 ml/4 fl oz milk

2 tbsp rum

finely grated rind and juice of 1 lime

pink sugar crystals, to decorate

Filling

350 g/12 oz fresh raspberries, puréed

55 g/2 oz caster sugar

2 tbsp rum

1 tbsp cornflour

Frosting

115 g/4 oz unsalted butter, softened

about 250 g/9 oz icing sugar (see method)

1 tsp raspberry extract

2 tbsp double cream

pinch of salt

Method

1 Preheat the oven to 180°C/350°F/Gas Mark 4 and line a 12-hole cupcake tin with paper cases.

2 Sift together the flour, baking powder and salt in a bowl. Put the butter and caster sugar into a separate bowl and beat until pale and fluffy. Add the eggs, one at a time, beating after each addition. Add half of the flour mixture, the milk, rum and lime rind and juice and beat until incorporated. Add the remaining flour mixture and mix.

3 Spoon the batter into the paper cases and bake in the preheated oven for 20 minutes, until risen and golden. Leave to cool in the tin for 1–2 minutes, then transfer to a wire rack to cool completely.

4 To make the filling, put the raspberry purée and caster sugar in a saucepan and bring to the boil, stirring frequently. Put the rum and cornflour into a small bowl and whisk together. Pour into the boiling raspberry mixture and cook for a further 1–2 minutes, stirring, until the mixture thickens. Remove from the heat and cool, then chill.

5 To make the frosting, use an electric mixer to beat the butter until it is pale and creamy. Add the remaining ingredients and 2 tablespoons of the raspberry filling. Beat together until

CUPCAKES & MUFFINS

well combined. Add more icing sugar, if necessary, to achieve a piping consistency. Spoon the frosting into a piping bag fitted with a star-shaped tip.

6 Use an apple corer to remove the centre of each cupcake and spoon the remaining raspberry filling into each hole. Pipe the frosting onto the cupcakes and then sprinkle with the sugar crystals.

TIRAMISÙ CUPCAKES

Makes: 12

Prep: 25 mins, plus cooling

Cook: 20-25 mins

Ingredients

115 g/4 oz unsalted butter, softened

115 g/4 oz soft light brown sugar

2 eggs, beaten

115 g/4 oz self-raising flour, sifted

½ tsp baking powder

2 tsp coffee granules

25 g/1 oz icing sugar

4 tbsp water

2 tbsp finely grated plain chocolate, for dusting

Frosting

225 g/8 oz mascarpone cheese

85 g/3 oz caster sugar

2 tbsp Marsala or sweet sherry

Method

1 Preheat the oven to 180°C/350°F/Gas Mark 4. Place 12 paper cases in a bun tin.

2 Place the butter, brown sugar, eggs, flour and baking powder in a bowl and beat together until pale and creamy. Divide the mixture evenly between the paper cases.

3 Bake the cupcakes in the preheated oven for 15–20 minutes, or until risen, golden and firm to the touch.

4 Place the coffee granules, icing sugar and water in a saucepan and heat gently, stirring, until the coffee and sugar have dissolved. Boil for 1 minute then leave to cool for 10 minutes. Brush the coffee syrup over the top of the warm cupcakes. Transfer the cupcakes to a wire rack and leave to cool.

5 For the frosting, put the mascarpone cheese, sugar and Marsala in a bowl and beat together until smooth. Spread over the top of the cakes. Using a star template, sprinkle the grated chocolate over the frosting.

IRISH COFFEE MUFFINS

Makes: 12

Prep: 25 mins,
plus cooling & chilling

Cook: 20 mins

Ingredients

280 g/10 oz plain flour

1 tbsp baking powder

pinch of salt

85 g/3 oz butter

55 g/2 oz soft light
brown sugar

1 large egg, beaten

125 ml/4 fl oz double cream

1 tsp almond extract

2 tbsp strong coffee

2 tbsp coffee-flavoured
liqueur

4 tbsp Irish whiskey

whipped cream and
cocoa powder, to serve
(optional)

Method

1 Preheat the oven to 200°C/400°F/Gas Mark 6.
Place 12 paper cases in a muffin tin. Sift
together the flour, baking powder and salt into
a large bowl.

2 In a separate large bowl, cream together the
butter and sugar, then stir in the egg. Mix in the
double cream, almond extract, coffee, liqueur
and whiskey. Make a well in the centre of the dry
ingredients and pour in the liquid ingredients. Stir
gently until just combined; do not over-mix.

3 Divide the mixture evenly between the
paper cases. Bake in the preheated oven for
20 minutes, or until well risen, golden brown and
firm to the touch.

4 Leave the muffins in the tin for 5 minutes, then
transfer to a wire rack and leave to cool. If liked,
pipe a swirl of whipped cream over the top of
each muffin and dust with cocoa powder. Chill
the muffins in the refrigerator until ready to serve

CHOCOLATE CHIP MUFFINS

Makes: 12

Prep: 20 mins, plus cooling

Cook: 25 mins

Ingredients

250 g/9 oz wholemeal self-raising flour

4 tbsp cocoa powder

70 g/2½ oz soft light brown sugar

100 g/3½ oz milk or plain chocolate chips

175 ml/6 fl oz reduced-fat Greek-style yogurt

200 ml/7 fl oz semi-skimmed milk

1 large egg

1 large ripe banana

50 g/1¾ oz butter

Method

1 Preheat the oven to 200°C/400°F/Gas Mark 6 and line a 12-cup muffin tin with paper cases. Sift the flour and cocoa powder into a bowl and stir in the sugar and chocolate chips.

2 Beat together the yogurt, milk and egg in another bowl. Mash the banana in a dish with a fork until almost liquid. Melt the butter in a saucepan over a low heat and stir into the banana. Add the banana mixture to the yogurt mixture and stir well.

3 Add the wet ingredients to the dry mixture and stir until just blended. Divide the mixture among the muffin cases and bake in the preheated oven for 20 minutes, until risen and just firm to the touch.

4 Leave the muffins in the tin for 5 minutes, then transfer to a wire rack to cool.

ICED CHOCOLATE ORANGE MUFFINS

Makes: 12

Prep: 25 mins, plus cooling

Cook: 25 mins

Ingredients

oil or melted butter, for greasing (if using)

2 oranges

about 125 ml/4 fl oz milk

225 g/8 oz plain flour

55 g/2 oz cocoa powder

1 tbsp baking powder

pinch of salt

115 g/4 oz soft light brown sugar

150 g/5½ oz plain chocolate chips

2 eggs

6 tbsp sunflower oil or 85 g/3 oz butter, melted and cooled

strips of orange zest, to decorate

Icing

55 g/2 oz plain chocolate, broken into pieces

25 g/1 oz butter

2 tbsp water

175 g/6 oz icing sugar

Method

1 Preheat the oven to 200°C/400°F/Gas Mark 6. Grease a 12-cup muffin tin or line with 12 paper cases. Finely grate the rind from the oranges and squeeze the juice. Transfer the juice to a measuring jug and add enough of the milk to make up to 250 ml/9 fl oz. Stir in the orange rind.

2 Sift together the flour, cocoa powder, baking powder and salt into a separate large bowl. Stir in the brown sugar and chocolate chips.

3 Lightly beat the eggs in a large jug, then beat in the milk and orange mixture and the oil. Make a well in the centre of the dry ingredients and pour in the beaten liquid ingredients. Stir gently until just combined; do not over-mix.

4 Spoon the mixture into the prepared muffin tin. Bake in the preheated oven for about 20 minutes, until well risen and firm to the touch.

5 Leave the muffins in the tin for 5 minutes, then transfer to a wire rack and leave to cool.

6 To make the icing, put the chocolate, butter and water in a heatproof bowl set over a saucepan of gently simmering water. Stir constantly, until melted. Remove from the heat, sift in the icing sugar and beat until smooth. While the icing is still warm, spread it on top of the muffins, then decorate with strips of orange zest.

CUPCAKES & MUFFINS

TRIPLE CHOCOLATE CHIP MUFFINS

Makes: 12

Prep: 20 mins, plus cooling

Cook: 20 mins

Ingredients

oil or melted butter, for greasing (if using)

280 g/10 oz plain flour

1 tbsp baking powder

pinch of salt

115 g/4 oz soft light brown sugar

50 g/1¾ oz plain chocolate chips

50 g/1¾ oz milk chocolate chips

50 g/1¾ oz white chocolate chips

2 eggs

250 ml/9 fl oz soured cream

6 tbsp sunflower oil or 85 g/3 oz butter, melted and cooled

1 tsp vanilla extract

Method

1 Preheat the oven to 200°C/400°F/Gas Mark 6. Grease a 12-cup muffin tin or line with 12 paper cases. Sift together the flour, baking powder and salt into a large bowl. Stir in the sugar and chocolate chips.

2 Lightly beat the eggs in a large jug, then beat in the soured cream, oil and vanilla extract. Make a well in the centre of the dry ingredients and pour in the beaten liquid ingredients. Stir gently until just combined; do not over-mix.

3 Spoon the mixture into the prepared muffin tin. Bake in the preheated oven for about 20 minutes, until well risen, golden brown and firm to the touch.

4 Leave the muffins in the tin for 5 minutes, then serve warm or transfer to a wire rack and leave to cool.

BERRY MUFFINS

Makes: 12

Prep: 20 mins,
plus optional cooling

Cook: 20–25 mins

Ingredients

225 g/8 oz plain flour

2 tsp baking powder

55 g/2 oz ground almonds

125 g/4½ oz caster sugar,
plus extra for sprinkling

150 g/5½ oz butter, melted

100 ml/3½ fl oz milk

2 eggs, beaten

250 g/9 oz mixed berries,
such as blueberries,
raspberries, blackberries
and redcurrants

Method

1 Preheat the oven to 190°C/375°F/Gas Mark 5.
   Place 12 paper cases in a muffin tin.

2 Sift together the flour and baking powder
   into a large bowl and stir in the ground almonds
   and sugar. Make a well in the centre of the
   dry ingredients.

3 Beat together the butter, milk and eggs and
   pour into the well. Stir gently until just combined;
   do not over-mix. Gently fold in the berries.

4 Divide the mixture evenly between the paper
   cases. Bake in the preheated oven for 20–25
   minutes, or until light golden and just firm to the
   touch. Serve warm or cold, sprinkled with sugar.

BLUEBERRY & VANILLA MUFFINS

Makes: 18

Prep: 30 mins, plus cooling

Cook: 15 mins

Ingredients

125 g/4½ oz self-raising flour
½ tsp baking powder
70 g/2½ oz caster sugar
85 g/3 oz blueberries
2 tsp vanilla extract
1 egg
125 ml/4 fl oz buttermilk
2 tbsp vegetable oil
vanilla sugar, plus extra for dusting

Method

1 Preheat the oven to 190°C/375°F/Gas Mark 5. Cut out eighteen 9-cm/3½-inch squares from baking paper. Push the squares into two 12-section mini muffin tins, creasing the squares to fit so that they form paper cases. Don't worry if they lift out of the sections slightly; the weight of the muffin mixture will hold them in place.

2 Sift the flour and baking powder into a mixing bowl. Stir in the sugar and blueberries. In a separate mixing bowl, beat together the vanilla, egg, buttermilk and oil with a fork until evenly combined.

3 Tip the buttermilk mixture into the flour. Using a dessertspoon, gently fold the ingredients together until only just mixed. (Don't over-blend the ingredients or the muffins won't be as light.)

4 Spoon the mixture into the paper cases; it should be level with the top of the tin. Sprinkle with a little vanilla sugar and bake in the preheated oven for 15 minutes, or until risen and just firm to the touch. Leave the muffins in the tin for 2 minutes, then transfer them in their cases to a wire rack to cool. Serve warm or cold, dusted with extra vanilla sugar.

CUPCAKES & MUFFINS

BLUEBERRY MUFFINS

Makes: 12

Prep: 20 mins,
plus cooling

Cook: 20 mins

Ingredients

280 g/10 oz plain flour

1 tbsp baking powder

pinch of salt

115 g/4 oz soft light
brown sugar

150 g/5½ oz frozen
blueberries

2 eggs

250 ml/9 fl oz milk

85 g/3 oz butter,
melted and cooled

1 tsp vanilla extract

finely grated rind of 1 lemon

Method

1 Preheat the oven to 200°C/400°F/Gas Mark 6.
Place 12 paper cases in a muffin tin. Sift together
the flour, baking powder and salt into a large
bowl. Stir in the sugar and blueberries.

2 Lightly beat the eggs in a large jug, then beat
in the milk, melted butter, vanilla extract and
lemon rind. Make a well in the centre of the
dry ingredients and pour in the beaten liquid
ingredients. Stir gently until just combined;
do not over-mix.

3 Divide the mixture evenly between the paper
cases. Bake in the preheated oven for about
20 minutes, or until well risen, golden brown and
firm to the touch.

4 Leave the muffins in the tin for 5 minutes, then
serve warm or transfer to a wire rack and leave
to cool.

CUPCAKES & MUFFINS

CHERRY & COCONUT MUFFINS

Makes: 12

Prep: 20 mins,
plus optional cooling

Cook: 20 mins

Ingredients

oil or melted butter,
for greasing (if using)

125 g/4½ oz glacé cherries

280 g/10 oz plain flour

1 tbsp baking powder

pinch of salt

115 g/4 oz caster sugar

40 g/1½ oz desiccated
coconut

2 eggs

250 ml/9 fl oz coconut milk

85 g/3 oz butter, melted
and cooled

1 tsp vanilla extract

12 whole fresh cherries
on their stalks

Method

1 Preheat the oven to 200°C/400°F/Gas Mark 6.
Grease a 12-cup muffin tin or line with 12 paper
cases. Cut the glacé cherries into small pieces.

2 Sift together the flour, baking powder and salt
into a large bowl. Stir in the sugar, desiccated
coconut and chopped glacé cherries.

3 Lightly beat the eggs in a large jug, then beat
in the coconut milk, melted butter and vanilla
extract. Make a well in the centre of the dry
ingredients and pour in the beaten liquid
ingredients. Stir gently until just combined;
do not over-mix.

4 Spoon the mixture into the prepared muffin tin.
Top each muffin with a whole fresh cherry. Bake
in the preheated oven for about 20 minutes, until
well risen, golden brown and firm to the touch.

5 Leave the muffins in the tin for 5 minutes, then
serve warm or transfer to a wire rack and leave
to cool.

FRESH STRAWBERRY & CREAM MUFFINS

Makes: 12

Prep: 25 mins,
plus cooling & chilling

Cook: 20 mins

Ingredients

oil or melted butter,
for greasing (if using)

150 g/5½ oz fresh
strawberries, plus extra
to decorate

280 g/10 oz plain flour

1 tbsp baking powder

pinch of salt

115 g/4 oz caster sugar

2 eggs

250 ml/9 fl oz single cream

6 tbsp sunflower oil or
85 g/3 oz butter,
melted and cooled

1 tsp vanilla extract

125 ml/4 fl oz double cream

Method

1 Preheat the oven to 200°C/400°F/Gas Mark 6.
Grease a 12-cup muffin tin or line with 12 paper
cases. Hull the strawberries and chop into
small pieces.

2 Sift together the flour, baking powder and salt
into a large bowl. Stir in the sugar and
chopped strawberries.

3 Lightly beat the eggs in a large jug, then beat in
the single cream, oil and vanilla extract. Make a
well in the centre of the dry ingredients and pour
in the beaten liquid ingredients. Stir gently until
just combined; do not over-mix.

4 Spoon the mixture into the prepared muffin
tin. Bake in the preheated oven for about
20 minutes, until well risen, golden brown and
firm to the touch.

5 Leave the muffins in the tin for 5 minutes, then
transfer to a wire rack and leave to cool.

6 Whisk the double cream until stiff. Place a
spoonful of the cream on top of each muffin,
then decorate with a whole strawberry. Chill the
muffins in the refrigerator until ready to serve.

RASPBERRY CRUMBLE MUFFINS

Makes: 12

Prep: 25 mins, plus cooling

Cook: 20 mins

Ingredients

oil or melted butter, for greasing (if using)
280 g/10 oz plain flour
1 tbsp baking powder
½ tsp bicarbonate of soda
pinch of salt
115 g/4 oz caster sugar
2 eggs
250 ml/9 fl oz natural yogurt
85 g/3 oz butter, melted and cooled
1 tsp vanilla extract
150 g/5½ oz frozen raspberries

Crumble topping

50 g/1¾ oz plain flour
35 g/1¼ oz butter
25 g/1 oz caster sugar

Method

1 Preheat the oven to 200°C/400°F/Gas Mark 6. Grease a 12-cup muffin tin or line with 12 paper cases.

2 To make the crumble topping, sift the flour into a bowl. Cut the butter into small pieces, add to the bowl and rub it in with your fingertips until the mixture resembles fine breadcrumbs. Stir in the sugar and set aside.

3 Sift together the flour, baking powder, bicarbonate of soda and salt into a large bowl. Stir in the sugar.

4 Lightly beat the eggs in a large jug, then beat in the yogurt, melted butter and vanilla extract. Make a well in the centre of the dry ingredients, pour in the beaten liquid ingredients and add the raspberries. Stir gently until just combined; do not over-mix.

5 Spoon the mixture into the prepared muffin tin. Scatter the crumble topping over the tops of the muffins and press down lightly. Bake in the preheated oven for about 20 minutes, until well risen, golden brown and firm to the touch.

6 Leave the muffins in the tin for 5 minutes, then serve warm or transfer to a wire rack and leave to cool.

WHITE CHOCOLATE & RASPBERRY MUFFINS

Makes: 12

Prep: 20 mins,
plus cooling

Cook: 20–25 mins

Ingredients

250 g/9 oz plain flour

1 tbsp baking powder

115 g/4 oz caster sugar

85 g/3 oz butter, chilled and roughly grated

1 large egg, beaten

175 ml/6 fl oz milk

175 g/6 oz raspberries

140 g/5 oz white chocolate chips

Method

1 Preheat the oven to 200°C/400°F/Gas Mark 6. Place 12 paper cases in a muffin tin.

2 Sift together the flour and baking powder into a large bowl and stir in the sugar. Add the butter and stir with a fork to coat in the flour mixture. Lightly beat the egg in a jug or bowl, then beat in the milk.

3 Make a well in the centre of the dry ingredients and pour in the beaten liquid ingredients. Stir gently until just combined; do not over-mix. Fold in the raspberries and half of the chocolate chips.

4 Divide the mixture evenly between the paper cases and scatter over the remaining chocolate chips. Bake in the preheated oven for 20–25 minutes, or until risen, golden and just firm to the touch. Leave to cool for 5 minutes, then transfer to a wire rack to cool completely.

★ **Variation**

Replace the raspberries with fresh or frozen blackberries, or try chopped fresh mango for a tropical flavour.

CHOCOLATE CHEESECAKE BROWNIES

Makes: 16

Prep: 25 mins, plus cooling

Cook: 50–55 mins

Ingredients

200 g/7 oz soft cheese

½ tsp vanilla extract

225 g/8 oz caster sugar

2 eggs

85 g/3 oz butter, plus extra for greasing

3 tbsp cocoa powder

100 g/3½ oz self-raising flour, sifted

50 g/1¾ oz pecan nuts, chopped, plus extra to decorate

Topping

55 g/2 oz butter

1 tbsp milk

75 g/2¾ oz icing sugar

2 tbsp cocoa powder

Method

1 Preheat the oven to 180°C/350°F/Gas Mark 4. Grease and line the base of a 20-cm/8-inch square cake tin. Beat together the soft cheese, vanilla extract and 5 teaspoons of the caster sugar until smooth, then set aside.

2 Beat together the eggs and the remaining caster sugar until light and fluffy. Place the butter and cocoa powder in a small saucepan and heat gently, stirring until the butter melts and the mixture combines, then stir it into the egg mixture. Fold in the flour and pecan nuts.

3 Pour half of the mixture into the prepared tin and smooth the top. Carefully spread the cheese mixture over it, then cover it with the remaining cake mixture. Bake in the preheated oven for 40–45 minutes. Leave to cool in the tin.

4 To make the topping, melt the butter in a small saucepan with the milk. Stir in the icing sugar and cocoa powder. Spread the topping over the brownies and decorate with pecan nuts. Leave the topping to set, then cut into squares to serve.

★ Variation

Place the brownies in sundae glasses with scoops of vanilla ice cream. Top with warm chocolate sauce.

SMALL BITES, COOKIES & BARS

CHOCOLATE & CHERRY BROWNIES

Makes: 12

Prep: 25 mins, plus cooling

Cook: 50–55 mins

Ingredients

175 g/6 oz plain chocolate, broken into pieces

175 g/6 oz butter, plus extra for greasing

225 g/8 oz caster sugar

3 large eggs, beaten

1 tsp vanilla extract

125 g/4½ oz self-raising flour

175 g/6 oz fresh cherries, stoned

85 g/3 oz white chocolate, roughly chopped

Method

1 Preheat the oven to 180°C/350°F/Gas Mark 4. Grease a 24 x 20-cm/9½ x 8-inch shallow cake tin and line with baking paper.

2 Put the plain chocolate and butter into a large, heatproof bowl set over a saucepan of simmering water and heat until melted. Remove from the heat and leave to cool for 5 minutes.

3 Beat the sugar, eggs and vanilla extract into the chocolate mixture. Sift in the flour and fold in gently. Pour the mixture into the prepared tin. Scatter over the cherries and the white chocolate.

4 Bake in the preheated oven for 30 minutes. Loosely cover the tops of the brownies with foil and bake for a further 15–20 minutes, or until just firm to the touch. Leave to cool in the tin, then cut into pieces.

CHOCOLATE SLABS

Makes: 12

Prep: 20 mins, plus cooling

Cook: 50–55 mins

Ingredients

200 g/7 oz butter, plus extra for greasing

100 g/3½ oz plain chocolate, broken into pieces

75 ml/2½ fl oz water

350 g/12 oz plain flour

2 tsp baking powder

250 g/9 oz soft light brown sugar

75 ml/2½ fl oz soured cream

2 eggs, beaten

Icing

200 g/7 oz plain chocolate, broken into pieces

6 tbsp water

3 tbsp single cream

15 g/½ oz butter, chilled

Method

1 Preheat the oven to 190°C/375°F/Gas Mark 5. Grease and line the base of a 23-cm/9-inch square cake tin.

2 Melt the butter and chocolate with the water in a saucepan over a low heat, stirring frequently. Sift the flour and baking powder into a mixing bowl and stir in the sugar. Pour in the chocolate mixture and beat well until all of the ingredients are evenly mixed. Stir in the soured cream, followed by the eggs.

3 Pour the mixture into the prepared cake tin and bake in the preheated oven for 40–45 minutes, until springy to the touch.

4 Leave the cake to cool slightly in the tin before turning it out onto a wire rack. Leave to cool completely.

5 To make the icing, melt the chocolate with the water in a saucepan over a very low heat, stir in the cream and remove from the heat. Stir in the butter, then pour the icing over the cooled cake, using a palette knife to spread it evenly over the top of the cake. Leave the icing to set and cut into twelve slabs.

S'MORE PIES

Makes: 12

Prep: 30 mins, plus cooling

Cook: 20 mins

Ingredients

40 g/1½ oz butter, plus extra for greasing

1 tbsp crunchy peanut butter

85 g/3 oz digestive biscuits or Rich Tea biscuits, crushed

100 g/3½ oz plain chocolate, roughly chopped

1 tbsp icing sugar

6 tbsp double cream

40 g/1½ oz mini marshmallows

Method

1 Preheat the oven to 180°C/350°F/Gas Mark 4. Lightly grease a 12-section mini muffin tin.

2 Put the butter in a small saucepan. Gently heat, uncovered, until it has melted. Take the saucepan off the heat and stir in the peanut butter, then the biscuit crumbs. Divide between the sections of the prepared tin. Press it firmly over the base and sides of the tin with the back of a teaspoon.

3 Bake in the preheated oven for 6 minutes, or until slightly darker in colour. Reshape the centre if needed with the back of a spoon. Leave to cool and harden in the tin for 10–15 minutes.

4 Meanwhile, put the chocolate in a heatproof bowl, set the bowl over a saucepan of gently simmering water and heat until melted. Add the sugar and gradually stir in the cream until smooth. Preheat the grill to medium.

5 Spoon the filling into the cases. Sprinkle the mini marshmallows over the top and press them lightly into the chocolate so they don't roll off.

6 Grill for 3–4 minutes, or until the marshmallows have softened and are just beginning to colour. Leave to cool in the tin for 30 minutes, then loosen with a round-bladed knife and carefully lift out of the tin. Serve.

SMALL BITES, COOKIES & BARS

HONEY & PISTACHIO DOUGHNUTS

Makes: 24

Prep: 30 mins,
plus cooling

Cook: 16–20 mins

Ingredients

115 g/4 oz self-raising flour

½ tsp baking powder

pinch of salt

55 g/2 oz butter, softened,
plus extra for greasing

55 g/2 oz caster sugar

1 egg, beaten

6 tbsp milk

40 g/1½ oz pistachio nuts,
finely chopped

Glaze

85 g/3 oz icing sugar

1 tbsp clear honey, warmed

2 tsp milk

Method

1 Preheat the oven to 190°C/375°F/Gas Mark 5. Grease a 12-hole mini doughnut tin. Sift together the flour, baking powder and salt into a bowl.

2 Put the butter and sugar into a separate bowl and beat together until pale and fluffy. Gradually beat in the egg, then stir in half the flour mixture. Beat in the milk, then fold in the remaining flour mixture and three quarters of the chopped nuts.

3 Spoon the mixture into a large, disposable piping bag. Snip off the end and pipe half the filling into the doughnut holes, filling each one about two-thirds full.

4 Bake in the preheated oven for 8–10 minutes, until risen, pale golden and just firm to the touch. Leave to cool in the tin for 2–3 minutes, then transfer to a wire rack. Bake the remaining mixture in the same way, rinsing and greasing the tin before filling.

5 To make the glaze, sift the icing sugar into a bowl and stir in the warm honey and milk to make a smooth glaze. Dip the top of each doughnut into the glaze then sprinkle with the remaining chopped nuts.

PEANUT BUTTER COOKIES

Makes: 15

Prep: 30 mins,
plus chilling & cooling

Cook: 15 mins

Ingredients

175 g/6 oz plain flour

½ tsp baking powder

½ tsp salt

225 g/8 oz smooth peanut butter

115 g/4 oz butter, softened

1¼ tsp vanilla extract

115 g/4 oz brown sugar

100 g/3½ oz caster sugar

2 eggs

Method

1 Sift together the flour, baking powder and salt into a bowl and set aside. Beat together the peanut butter, butter and vanilla extract until smooth in another bowl. Beat in the brown and caster sugars for 1 minute, then beat in the eggs one at a time. Stir in the flour mixture in two batches.

2 Halve the dough, shape into balls, wrap in clingfilm and chill in the refrigerator for at least 2 hours. Meanwhile, preheat the oven to 180°C/350°F/Gas Mark 4. Line two baking sheets with baking paper or leave uncovered and ungreased.

3 Roll or scoop the dough into 4-cm/1½-inch balls and place them on the prepared baking sheets, spaced well apart. Use a fork to flatten each ball by making a criss-cross pattern. Bake in the preheated oven for 15 minutes, or until golden. Remove the biscuits from the oven and leave to cool on the baking sheet for 5 minutes. Using a palette knife, transfer to a wire rack to cool completely.

SMALL BITES, COOKIES & BARS

VANILLA CAKE POPS

Makes: 24

Prep: 1–1¼ hours, plus chilling

Cook: 5 mins

Ingredients

450 g/1 lb ready-made vanilla sponge

85 g/3 oz mascarpone cheese

70 g/2½ oz icing sugar

½ tsp vanilla extract

Decoration

225 g/8 oz milk chocolate, roughly chopped

24 lolly sticks

150 g/5½ oz fondant icing sugar

pink food colouring

4 tsp cold water

24 small sweets, such as mini sugar-coated chocolate drops

sugar sprinkles

Method

1 Line a baking sheet with baking paper. Crumble the sponge cake into a mixing bowl. Add the mascarpone cheese, icing sugar and vanilla extract and mix together until you have a thick paste. Roll a 25-g/1-oz piece of the paste into a ball. Shape the remaining 23 cake pops in the same way. Place on the baking sheet and chill for 1–2 hours.

2 Put the chocolate in a heatproof bowl, set the bowl over a saucepan of gently simmering water and heat until melted. Remove from the heat. Push a lolly stick into each cake pop. Dip a cake pop into the chocolate, turning it until coated. Lift it from the bowl, letting the excess drip back into the bowl, then place it in a cup or tumbler. Repeat with the remaining cake pops. Chill or leave in a cool place until the chocolate has set.

3 Put the fondant icing sugar in a bowl and beat in a dash of pink food colouring and the water until smooth. The icing should almost hold its shape. Spoon a little onto a cake pop, easing it slightly down the sides with the side of a teaspoon. If the icing is too firm, add a dash more water. Before the icing sets, place a sweet in the centre of each cake pop and scatter with sugar sprinkles.

SMALL BITES, COOKIES & BARS

CHOCOLATE MINT CAKE POPS

Makes: 28

Prep: 50 mins, plus cooling & chilling

Cook: 10 mins

Ingredients

300 g/10½ oz plain chocolate, roughly chopped

25 g/1 oz unsalted butter, softened

50 g/1¾ oz hard-boiled mint sweets

450 g/1 lb milk chocolate

50 g/1¾ oz mini marshmallows, roughly chopped

28 lolly sticks

chocolate sprinkles, to decorate

Method

1 Line a baking sheet with baking paper. Put the plain chocolate in a heatproof bowl, set the bowl over a saucepan of gently simmering water and heat until melted. Stir in the butter. Leave until the mixture is cool but not beginning to set.

2 Put the mint sweets in a polythene bag and tap firmly with a rolling pin until they are broken into tiny pieces. Finely chop 150 g/5½ oz of the milk chocolate, then stir it into the melted plain chocolate with the mints and marshmallows until thoroughly mixed.

3 As soon as the mixture is firm enough to hold its shape, roll 20 g/¾ oz of it into a ball. Shape the remaining cake pops in the same way. Place them on the baking sheet and chill for 30–60 minutes, or until firm but not brittle. Push a lolly stick into each cake pop, then chill for 10 minutes.

4 Roughly chop the remaining milk chocolate and melt as above, then remove from the heat. Dip a cake pop into the chocolate, turning it until coated. Lift it from the bowl, letting the excess drip back into the bowl, and place it in a cup or tumbler. Sprinkle with chocolate sprinkles. Repeat with the remaining cake pops. Chill or leave in a cool place until the chocolate has set.

DOUBLE CHOCOLATE WHOOPIE PIES

Makes: 12

Prep: 35 mins, plus cooling & chilling

Cook: 20–25 mins

Ingredients

200 g/7 oz plain flour

1½ tsp bicarbonate of soda

25 g/1 oz cocoa powder

large pinch of salt

85 g/3 oz butter, softened

85 g/3 oz white vegetable fat

150 g/5½ oz soft light brown sugar

25 g/1 oz plain chocolate, finely grated

1 large egg, beaten

125 ml/4 fl oz milk

4 tbsp plain chocolate strands

White chocolate filling

175 g/6 oz white chocolate, broken into pieces

2 tbsp milk

300 ml/10 fl oz double cream

Method

1 Preheat the oven to 180°C/350°F/Gas Mark 4. Line 2–3 large baking sheets with baking paper. Sift together the plain flour, bicarbonate of soda, cocoa powder and salt.

2 Place the butter, white vegetable fat, sugar and grated chocolate in a large bowl and beat with an electric handheld whisk until pale and fluffy. Beat in the egg followed by half the flour mixture then the milk. Stir in the rest of the flour mixture and mix until thoroughly incorporated.

3 Pipe or spoon 24 mounds of the mixture onto the prepared baking sheets, spaced well apart to allow for spreading. Bake in the preheated oven, one sheet at a time, for 10–12 minutes, or until risen and just firm to the touch. Cool for 5 minutes then, using a palette knife, transfer to a wire rack and leave to cool completely.

4 For the filling, place the chocolate and milk in a heatproof bowl set over a saucepan of simmering water. Heat until the chocolate has melted, stirring occasionally. Remove from the heat and leave to cool for 30 minutes. Using an electric whisk, whip the cream until holding firm peaks. Fold in the chocolate. Cover and chill in the refrigerator for 30–45 minutes, or until firm enough to spread.

SMALL BITES, COOKIES & BARS

To assemble, spread or pipe the chocolate filling on the flat side of half of the cakes. Top with the rest of the cakes. Spread the chocolate strands on a plate and gently roll the edges of each whoopie pie in the strands to lightly coat.

CHOCOLATE COOKIE SANDWICHES

Makes: 15   **Prep: 35 mins,** plus cooling   **Cook: 15–20 mins**

Ingredients

225 g/8 oz butter, softened

140 g/5 oz caster sugar

2 tsp finely grated orange rind

1 egg yolk, lightly beaten

2 tsp vanilla extract

250 g/9 oz plain flour

25 g/1 oz cocoa powder

pinch of salt

100 g/3½ oz plain chocolate, finely chopped

Chocolate filling

125 ml/4 fl oz double cream

200 g/7 oz white chocolate, broken into pieces

1 tsp orange extract

Method

1 Preheat the oven to 190°C/375°F/Gas Mark 5. Line 2 baking sheets with baking paper.

2 Put the butter, sugar and orange rind into a bowl and mix well with a wooden spoon, then beat in the egg yolk and vanilla extract. Sift together the flour, cocoa powder and salt into the mixture, add the plain chocolate and stir until thoroughly combined.

3 Scoop up tablespoons of the dough, roll into balls and place on the prepared baking sheets, spaced well apart. Gently flatten and smooth the tops with the back of a spoon. Bake in the preheated oven for 10–15 minutes, until light golden brown. Leave to cool on the baking sheets for 5–10 minutes, then, using a palette knife, carefully transfer to wire racks to cool completely.

4 To make the filling, bring the cream to the boil in a small saucepan, then remove the pan from the heat. Stir in the white chocolate until the mixture is smooth, then stir in the orange extract. When the mixture is completely cool, use to sandwich the cookies together in pairs.

VANILLA WHOOPIE PIES

Makes: 12

Prep: 35 mins,
plus cooling

Cook: 20–30 mins

Ingredients

250 g/9 oz plain flour

1 tsp bicarbonate of soda

large pinch of salt

175 g/6 oz butter, softened

150 g/5½ oz caster sugar

1 large egg, beaten

2 tsp vanilla extract

150 ml/5 fl oz buttermilk

Chocolate buttercream filling

115 g/4 oz milk chocolate, broken into pieces

115 g/4 oz unsalted butter, softened

250 g/9 oz icing sugar, sifted

Method

1 Preheat the oven to 180°C/350°F/Gas Mark 4. Line 2–3 large baking sheets with baking paper. Sift together the plain flour, bicarbonate of soda and salt.

2 Place the butter and sugar in a large bowl and beat until pale and fluffy. Beat in the egg and vanilla extract followed by half the flour mixture and then the buttermilk. Stir in the rest of the flour mixture and mix until thoroughly incorporated.

3 Pipe or spoon 24 mounds of the mixture onto the prepared baking sheets, spaced well apart to allow for spreading. Bake in the oven, one sheet at a time, for 10–12 minutes, or until risen and just firm to the touch. Cool for 5 minutes then, using a palette knife, transfer to a wire rack and leave to cool completely.

4 For the filling, place the chocolate in a heatproof bowl set over a saucepan of simmering water and leave to melt. Remove from the heat and leave to cool for 20 minutes, stirring occasionally. Place the butter in a bowl and beat with an electric whisk for 2–3 minutes, or until pale and creamy. Gradually beat in the icing sugar then beat in the chocolate. To assemble, pipe the buttercream on the flat side of half of the cakes. Top with the rest of the cakes.

GIANT CHOCOLATE CHUNK COOKIES

Makes: 12

Prep: 20 mins,
plus cooling

Cook: 15–20 mins

Ingredients

115 g/4 oz butter, softened

125 g/4½ oz caster sugar

125 g/4½ oz soft light brown sugar

2 large eggs, lightly beaten

1 tsp vanilla extract

280 g/10 oz plain flour

1 tsp bicarbonate of soda

300 g/10½ oz chocolate chunks

Method

1 Preheat the oven to 180°C/350°F/Gas Mark 4. Line 3–4 large baking sheets with baking paper.

2 Place the butter and sugars in a large bowl and beat together until pale and creamy. Whisk the eggs and vanilla extract into the mixture until smooth. Sift in the flour and bicarbonate of soda and beat together until well mixed. Stir in the chocolate chunks.

3 Drop 12 large spoonfuls of the mixture onto the prepared baking sheets, spaced well apart.

4 Bake in the preheated oven for 15–20 minutes, or until set and golden brown. Leave to cool on the baking sheets for 2–3 minutes, then transfer the cookies to a wire rack to cool completely.

SMALL BITES, COOKIES & BARS

SNICKERDOODLE WHOOPIE PIES

Makes: 15

Prep: 40 mins, plus cooling

Cook: 20–30 mins

Ingredients

250 g/9 oz plain flour

1 tsp bicarbonate of soda

large pinch of salt

2 tsp ground cinnamon

115 g/4 oz butter, softened

150 g/5½ oz caster sugar, plus 2 tbsp for sprinkling

1 large egg, beaten

1 tsp vanilla extract

150 ml/5 fl oz buttermilk

Coffee filling

115 g/4 oz unsalted butter, softened

85 g/3 oz full-fat soft cheese

1 tbsp strong cold black coffee

280 g/10 oz icing sugar, sifted

Method

1 Preheat the oven to 180°C/350°F/Gas Mark 4. Line 2–3 large baking sheets with baking paper. Sift together the flour, bicarbonate of soda, salt and 1 teaspoon of the cinnamon.

2 Place the butter and the 150 g/5½ oz caster sugar in a large bowl and beat with an electric handheld whisk until pale and fluffy. Beat in the egg and vanilla extract followed by half the flour mixture and then the buttermilk. Stir in the rest of the flour mixture and mix until thoroughly incorporated.

3 Pipe or spoon 30 mounds of the mixture onto the prepared baking sheets, spaced well apart to allow for spreading. Mix together the rest of the cinnamon with the 2 tablespoons of caster sugar and sprinkle liberally over the mounds. Bake in the oven, one sheet at a time, for 10–12 minutes, or until just risen and just firm to the touch. Cool for 5 minutes then, using a palette knife, transfer to a wire rack and leave to cool.

4 For the filling, place the butter, soft cheese and coffee in a bowl and beat together until well blended. Gradually beat in the icing sugar until smooth. To assemble, spread or pipe the coffee filling on the flat side of half of the cakes. Top with the rest of the cakes.

SMALL BITES, COOKIES & BARS

SUGAR COOKIES

Makes: 20

Prep: 25 mins,
plus chilling & cooling

Cook: 10–12 mins

Ingredients

115 g/4 oz butter, softened, plus extra for greasing

55 g/2 oz caster sugar, plus extra for sprinkling

1 tsp finely grated lemon rind

1 egg yolk

175 g/6 oz plain flour, plus extra for dusting

Method

1 Place the butter and sugar in a bowl and beat together until pale and creamy. Beat in the lemon rind and egg yolk. Sift in the flour and mix to a soft dough. Turn out onto a floured work surface and knead until smooth, adding a little more flour if necessary. Halve the dough, shape into balls, wrap in clingfilm and chill in the refrigerator for 1 hour.

2 Preheat the oven to 180°C/350°F/Gas Mark 4. Lightly grease two large baking sheets.

3 Roll out the dough on a lightly floured work surface to a thickness of 5 mm/¼ inch. Using 7-cm/2 ¾-inch flower-shaped and heart-shaped cutters stamp out 20 cookies, re-rolling the dough as necessary. Place on the prepared baking sheets and sprinkle with sugar.

4 Bake in the preheated oven for 10–12 minutes, or until pale golden. Leave to cool on the baking sheets for 2–3 minutes, then transfer to a wire rack to cool completely.

MARSHMALLOW S'MORES

Makes: 15

Prep: 45 mins,
plus chilling & cooling

Cook: 16–22 mins

Ingredients

225 g/8 oz butter, softened

140 g/5 oz caster sugar

2 tsp finely grated orange rind

1 egg yolk, lightly beaten

250 g/9 oz plain flour

25 g/1 oz cocoa powder

½ tsp ground cinnamon

pinch of salt

30 marshmallows, halved horizontally

300 g/10½ oz plain chocolate, broken into pieces

4 tbsp orange marmalade

15 walnut halves, to decorate

Method

1 Place the butter, sugar and orange rind in a large bowl and beat together until light and fluffy, then beat in the egg yolk. Sift together the flour, cocoa, cinnamon and salt into the mixture and stir until combined. Halve the dough, shape into balls, wrap in clingfilm and chill for 30–60 minutes.

2 Preheat the oven to 190°C/375°F/Gas Mark 5. Line several large baking sheets with baking paper. Unwrap the dough and roll out between two sheets of baking paper. Cut out 30 cookies with a 6-cm/2½-inch fluted round cutter and place them on the prepared baking sheets, spaced well apart. Bake in the oven for 10–15 minutes. Leave to cool for 5 minutes. Turn half the cookies upside down and put four marshmallow halves on each. Bake these cookies for a further 1–2 minutes. Leave the cookies on wire racks for 30 minutes.

3 Place the chocolate in a heatproof bowl, set the bowl over a saucepan of gently simmering water and heat until melted. Line a baking sheet with baking paper. Spread the marmalade over the undersides of the uncovered cookies and place them on top of the marshmallow-covered cookies. Dip the cookies in the melted chocolate. Place a walnut half in the centre of each cookie and leave to set.

SMALL BITES, COOKIES & BARS

GINGERNUTS

Makes: 30

Prep: 25 mins,
plus cooling

Cook: 15–20 mins

Ingredients

350 g/12 oz self-raising flour

pinch of salt

200 g/7 oz caster sugar

1 tbsp ground ginger

1 tsp bicarbonate of soda

125 g/4½ oz butter,
plus extra for greasing

75 g/2¾ oz golden syrup

1 egg, beaten

1 tsp grated orange rind

Method

1 Preheat the oven to 160°C/325°F/Gas Mark 3.
Lightly grease several baking sheets.

2 Sift together the flour, salt, sugar, ginger and
bicarbonate of soda into a large mixing bowl.

3 Heat the butter and golden syrup together in a
saucepan over a very low heat until the butter
has melted. Remove the pan from the heat and
leave to cool slightly, then pour the contents
onto the dry ingredients.

4 Add the egg and orange rind and mix
thoroughly with a wooden spoon to form a
dough. Using your hands, carefully shape the
dough into 30 even-sized balls. Place the balls on
the prepared baking sheets, spaced well apart,
then flatten them slightly with your fingers.

5 Bake in the preheated oven for 15–20 minutes,
then carefully transfer to a wire rack to
cool completely.

RASPBERRY MACAROONS

Makes: 16

Prep: 45 mins,
plus resting & cooling

Cook: 10–15 mins

Ingredients

75 g/2¾ oz ground almonds
115 g/4 oz icing sugar
2 large egg whites
50 g/1¾ oz caster sugar
pink food colouring

Filling

150 ml/5 fl oz double cream
1 tsp vanilla extract
3 tbsp raspberry jam

Method

1 Place the ground almonds and icing sugar in a food processor and process for 15 seconds. Sift the mixture into a bowl. Line two baking sheets with baking paper. Place the egg whites in a large bowl and whisk until holding soft peaks. Gradually whisk in the caster sugar to make a firm, glossy meringue. Whisk in food colouring until bright pink.

2 Using a spatula, fold the almond mixture into the meringue one third at a time. When all the dry ingredients are thoroughly incorporated, continue to cut and fold the mixture until it forms a shiny batter with a thick, ribbon-like consistency.

3 Pour the mixture into a piping bag fitted with a 1-cm/½-inch plain nozzle. Pipe 32 small rounds onto the prepared baking sheets. Tap the baking sheets firmly onto a work surface to remove air bubbles. Use the tip of a cocktail stick to swirl a little food colouring through the top of each macaroon. Leave at room temperature for 30 minutes. Preheat the oven to 160°C/325°F/ Gas Mark 3. Bake in the preheated oven for 10–15 minutes. Cool for 10 minutes, then carefully peel the macaroons off the baking paper. Leave to cool completely.

4 To make the filling, whip the cream and vanilla extract together until holding soft peaks. Sandwich pairs of macaroons together with the vanilla cream and jam.

BISCOTTI

Makes: 30

Prep: 25 mins,
plus chilling & cooling

Cook: 10 mins

Ingredients

225 g/8 oz butter, softened
140 g/5 oz caster sugar
finely grated rind of 1 lemon
1 egg yolk, lightly beaten
2 tsp brandy
280 g/10 oz plain flour
pinch of salt
85 g/3 oz pistachio nuts
icing sugar, for dusting

Method

1 Put the butter, caster sugar and lemon rind into a bowl and mix well with a wooden spoon, then beat in the egg yolk and brandy. Sift together the flour and salt into the mixture and stir in the pistachio nuts until thoroughly combined.

2 Shape the mixture into a log, flatten slightly, wrap in clingfilm and chill in the refrigerator for 30–60 minutes.

3 Preheat the oven to 190°C/375°F/Gas Mark 5. Line two baking sheets with baking paper. Unwrap the log and cut it slightly on the diagonal into 5-mm/¼-inch slices with a sharp serrated knife. Put them on the prepared baking sheets, spaced well apart.

4 Bake in the preheated oven for 10 minutes, or until golden brown. Leave to cool on the baking sheets for 5–10 minutes, then, using a palette knife, carefully transfer to wire racks to cool completely. Dust with icing sugar.

CLASSIC OATMEAL COOKIES

Makes: 30

Prep: 20 mins,
plus cooling

Cook: 15 mins

Ingredients

175 g/6 oz butter, softened,
plus extra for greasing

275 g/9¾ oz demerara
sugar

1 egg, beaten

4 tbsp water

1 tsp vanilla extract

375 g/13 oz rolled oats

140 g/5 oz plain flour

1 tsp salt

½ tsp bicarbonate of soda

Method

1 Preheat the oven to 180°C/350°F/Gas Mark 4.
  Grease two large baking sheets.

2 Place the butter and sugar in a large bowl and
  beat together until pale and creamy. Beat in the
  egg, water and vanilla extract until the mixture is
  smooth. Mix the oats, flour, salt and bicarbonate
  of soda together in a separate bowl, then
  gradually stir the oat mixture into the creamed
  mixture until thoroughly combined.

3 Place tablespoonfuls of the mixture on the
  prepared baking sheets, spaced well apart.

4 Bake in the preheated oven for 15 minutes,
  or until golden brown. Transfer to a wire rack to
  cool completely.

DOUBLE CHOCOLATE PECAN BLONDIES

Makes: 12

Prep: 30 mins, plus cooling

Cook: 35–40 mins

Ingredients

250 g/9 oz white chocolate, broken into pieces

40 g/1½ oz butter, plus extra for greasing

175 g/6 oz plain chocolate

2 large eggs, beaten

85 g/3 oz caster sugar

115 g/4 oz self-raising flour

100 g/3½ oz pecan nuts, roughly chopped

Method

1 Preheat the oven to 180°C/350°F/Gas Mark 4. Grease a 20-cm/8-inch shallow square baking tin or baking dish.

2 Place 85 g/3 oz of the white chocolate in a heatproof bowl and add the butter. Set the bowl over a saucepan of gently simmering water and heat, stirring occasionally, until melted and smooth. Meanwhile, roughly chop the remaining white and plain chocolate.

3 Beat the eggs and sugar together in a large bowl then stir in the melted chocolate mixture. Sift the flour over the top. Add the chopped chocolate and pecan nuts. Mix well.

4 Spoon the mixture into the prepared tin and smooth the surface. Bake in the preheated oven for 35–40 minutes, or until golden brown and just firm to the touch in the centre. Leave in the tin until completely cooled and the chocolate chunks inside have set, then turn out and cut into pieces.

CARAMEL CHOCOLATE SHORTBREAD

Makes: 12

Prep: 30 mins,
plus chilling & cooling

Cook: 25–30 mins

Ingredients

115 g/4 oz unsalted butter,
plus extra for greasing

175 g/6 oz plain flour

55 g/2 oz golden caster
sugar

Filling & topping

200 g/7 oz butter

115 g/4 oz golden caster
sugar

3 tbsp golden syrup

400 g/14 oz canned
condensed milk

200 g/7 oz plain chocolate,
broken into pieces

Method

1 Preheat the oven to 180°C/350°F/Gas Mark 4.
Grease and line the base of a 23-cm/9-inch
square shallow cake tin.

2 Place the butter, flour and sugar in a food
processor and process until they begin to bind
together. Press the mixture into the prepared
tin and smooth the top. Bake in the preheated oven
for 20–25 minutes, or until golden.

3 Meanwhile, make the filling. Place the butter,
sugar, golden syrup and condensed milk in a
saucepan and heat gently until the sugar has
dissolved. Bring to the boil and simmer for
6–8 minutes, stirring constantly, until the mixture
becomes very thick. Remove the shortbread
base from the oven, pour over the filling and
chill in the refrigerator until firm.

4 To make the topping, melt the chocolate in a
heatproof bowl set over a saucepan of gently
simmering water. Remove from the heat, leave to
cool slightly, then spread over the caramel. Chill
in the refrigerator until set. Cut into 12 pieces with
a sharp knife and serve.

DATE, PISTACHIO & HONEY SLICES

Makes: 12

Prep: 35 mins, plus cooling

Cook: 25–30 mins

Ingredients

250 g/9 oz dates, stoned and chopped

2 tbsp lemon juice

2 tbsp water

85 g/3 oz pistachio nuts, chopped

2 tbsp clear honey

milk, to glaze

Pastry

225 g/8 oz plain flour, plus extra for dusting

25 g/1 oz golden caster sugar

150 g/5½ oz butter

4–5 tbsp cold water, to mix

Method

1 Place the dates, lemon juice and water in a saucepan and bring to the boil, stirring. Remove from the heat. Stir in the pistachio nuts and 1 tablespoon of honey. Cover and leave to cool.

2 Preheat the oven to 200°C/400°F/Gas Mark 6. For the pastry, place the flour, sugar and butter in a food processor and process to fine crumbs. Mix in just enough cold water to bind to a soft, not sticky, dough.

3 Roll out the pastry on a floured surface to two 30 x 20-cm/12 x 8-inch rectangles. Place one on a baking sheet. Spread the date and nut mixture to within 1 cm/½ inch of the edge. Top with the remaining pastry.

4 Press to seal, trim the edges and mark into 12 slices. Glaze with the milk. Bake in the preheated oven for 20–25 minutes, or until golden. Brush with the remaining honey and turn out onto a wire rack to cool. Cut into slices and serve.

COCONUT BARS

Makes: 10

Prep: 25 mins,
plus cooling

Cook: 35–40 mins

Ingredients

125 g/4½ oz unsalted butter, plus extra for greasing

225 g/8 oz golden caster sugar

2 eggs, beaten

finely grated rind of 1 orange

3 tbsp orange juice

150 ml/5 fl oz soured cream

140 g/5 oz self-raising flour

85 g/3 oz desiccated coconut

toasted shredded coconut, to decorate

Frosting

1 egg white

200 g/7 oz icing sugar

85 g/3 oz desiccated coconut

about 1 tbsp orange juice

Method

1 Preheat the oven to 180°C/350°F/Gas Mark 4. Grease a 23-cm/9-inch square cake tin and line the base with non-stick baking paper.

2 Cream together the butter and caster sugar until pale and fluffy, then gradually beat in the eggs. Stir in the orange rind, orange juice and soured cream. Fold in the flour and desiccated coconut evenly using a metal spoon.

3 Spoon the mixture into the prepared cake tin and level the surface. Bake in the preheated oven for 35–40 minutes, or until risen and firm to the touch.

4 Leave to cool for 10 minutes in the tin, then turn out and finish cooling on a wire rack.

5 For the frosting, lightly beat the egg white, and stir in the icing sugar and desiccated coconut, adding enough orange juice to mix to a thick paste. Spread over the top of the cake, sprinkle with toasted shredded coconut, then leave to set before slicing into bars.

CHOCOLATE PEPPERMINT BARS

Makes: 16

Prep: 30 mins,
plus cooling & setting

Cook: 15–20 mins

Ingredients

55 g/2 oz unsalted butter,
plus extra for greasing

55 g/2 oz caster sugar

115 g/4 oz plain flour

Filling & topping

175 g/6 oz icing sugar

1–2 tbsp warm water

½ tsp peppermint extract

2 tsp green edible food
colouring (optional)

175 g/6 oz plain chocolate,
broken into pieces

Method

1 Preheat the oven to 180°C/350°F/Gas Mark 4.
   Grease and line the base of a 30 x 20-cm/
   12 x 8-inch baking tin.

2 Beat the butter and caster sugar together until
   pale and fluffy. Stir in the flour until the mixture
   binds together.

3 Knead the mixture to form a smooth dough, then
   press into the prepared tin. Prick the surface all
   over with a fork. Bake in the preheated oven for
   10–15 minutes, until lightly browned and just firm
   to the touch. Remove from the oven and leave
   to cool in the tin.

4 For the filling, sift the icing sugar into a bowl.
   Gradually add the water, then add the
   peppermint extract and food colouring, if using.
   Spread the filling over the base, then leave to set.

5 Melt the chocolate in a heatproof bowl set over
   a saucepan of gently simmering water, remove
   from the heat, then spread over the filling. Leave
   to set, then cut into slices.

SMALL BITES, COOKIES & BARS

RAISIN FLAPJACKS

Makes: 14

Prep: 15 mins, plus cooling

Cook: 15-20 mins

Ingredients

140 g/5 oz rolled oats

115 g/4 oz demerara sugar

85 g/3 oz raisins

115 g/4 oz butter, melted, plus extra for greasing

Method

1 Preheat the oven to 190°C/375°F/Gas Mark 5. Grease a 28 x 18-cm/11 x 7-inch shallow baking tin.

2 Combine the oats, sugar and raisins with the butter in a mixing bowl, stirring well. Spoon the mixture into the prepared tin and press down firmly with the back of a spoon. Bake in the preheated oven for 15–20 minutes, or until golden.

3 Using a sharp knife, mark into 14 bars, then leave to cool in the tin for 10 minutes. Carefully transfer the bars to a wire rack to cool completely.

APRICOT FLAPJACKS

Makes: 10

Prep: 20 mins, plus cooling

Cook: 25–30 mins

Ingredients

175 g/6 oz margarine, plus extra for greasing

85 g/3 oz demerara sugar

55 g/2 oz clear honey

140 g/5 oz dried apricots, chopped

2 tsp sesame seeds

225 g/8 oz rolled oats

Method

1 Preheat the oven to 180°C/350°F/Gas Mark 4. Grease a 26 x 17-cm/10½ x 6½-inch shallow baking tin.

2 Put the margarine, sugar and honey into a small saucepan over a low heat and heat until the ingredients have melted together – do not boil. When the ingredients are well combined, stir in the apricots, sesame seeds and oats.

3 Spoon the mixture into the prepared tin and smooth the surface with the back of a spoon. Bake in the preheated oven for 20–25 minutes, or until golden brown.

4 Remove from the oven, cut into ten bars and leave to cool completely before removing from the tin.

CHOCOLATE & NUT OAT COOKIES

Makes: 15

Prep: 20 mins, plus cooling

Cook: 15–20 mins

Ingredients

85 g/3 oz unsalted butter, plus extra for greasing

175 g/6 oz chocolate hazelnut spread

175 g/6 oz porridge oats

70 g/2½ oz blanched hazelnuts, chopped

Method

1 Preheat the oven to 200°C/400°F/Gas Mark 6. Grease a baking sheet.

2 Place the butter and chocolate hazelnut spread in a saucepan and heat gently until just melted.

3 Add the porridge oats and hazelnuts to the chocolate mixture and stir to combine thoroughly.

4 Shape the mixture into 15 equal-sized balls, then press onto the prepared baking sheet. Bake in the preheated oven for 10–12 minutes. Remove from the oven and leave until firm before transferring the cookies to a wire rack to finish cooling.

ROCKY ROAD BARS

Makes: 8

Prep: 20 mins,
plus cooling & chilling

Cook: 5 mins

Ingredients

175 g/6 oz milk or plain chocolate

55 g/2 oz butter

100 g/3½ oz shortcake biscuits, broken into pieces

85 g/3 oz mini marshmallows

85 g/3 oz walnuts or peanuts

Method

1 Break the chocolate into squares and place in a heatproof bowl set over a saucepan of gently simmering water and heat until melted. Add the butter and stir until melted and combined. Leave to cool slightly.

2 Stir the broken biscuits, marshmallows and nuts into the chocolate mixture.

3 Line an 18-cm/7-inch square cake tin with baking paper and pour in the chocolate mixture, pressing down with the back of a spoon.

4 Chill in the refrigerator for at least 2 hours, or until firm. Carefully turn out of the tin and cut into eight pieces.

★ Variation

Add some chopped glacé cherries or dried apricots for a fruity flavour.

CAKES

CLASSIC CHOCOLATE CAKE

Serves: 10

Prep: 35 mins,
plus cooling & chilling

Cook: 30–35 mins

Ingredients

55 g/2 oz cocoa powder

7 tbsp boiling water

200 g/7 oz butter, softened, plus extra for greasing

125 g/4½ oz caster sugar

70 g/2½ oz soft light brown sugar

4 eggs, beaten

1 tsp vanilla extract

200 g/7 oz self-raising flour

Frosting

200 g/7 oz plain chocolate, broken into pieces

115 g/4 oz unsalted butter

100 ml/3½ fl oz double cream

Method

1 Preheat the oven to 180°C/350°F/Gas Mark 4. Grease two 20-cm/8-inch sandwich tins and line with baking paper. Blend the cocoa powder and water to a smooth paste and set aside. Put the butter, caster sugar and brown sugar into a large bowl and beat together until pale and creamy. Gradually beat in the eggs, then stir in the cocoa paste and vanilla extract.

2 Sift in the flour and fold in gently. Divide the mixture between the prepared tins. Bake in the preheated oven for 25–30 minutes, or until risen and just springy to the touch. Leave to cool in the tins for 5 minutes, then leave on a rack to cool.

3 To make the frosting, put the chocolate and butter into a heatproof bowl set over a saucepan of simmering water, and heat until melted. Remove from the heat and stir in the cream. Leave to cool for 20 minutes, then chill in the refrigerator for 40–50 minutes, stirring occasionally, until thick enough to spread. Sandwich the sponges together with one third of the frosting, then spread the remainder over the top of the cake.

★ **Variation**

Try white chocolate frosting for a contrast.

CAKES

CHOCOLATE FUDGE CAKE

Serves: 8

Prep: 35 mins, plus cooling & chilling

Cook: 35–40 mins

Ingredients

175 g/6 oz unsalted butter, softened, plus extra for greasing

175 g/6 oz golden caster sugar

3 eggs, beaten

3 tbsp golden syrup

40 g/1½ oz ground almonds

175 g/6 oz self-raising flour

pinch of salt

40 g/1½ oz cocoa powder

Icing

225 g/8 oz plain chocolate, broken into pieces

55 g/2 oz dark muscovado sugar

225 g/8 oz unsalted butter, diced

5 tbsp evaporated milk

½ tsp vanilla extract

Method

1 Preheat the oven to 180°C/350°F/Gas Mark 4. Grease and line two 20-cm/8-inch sandwich tins.

2 For the icing, place the ingredients in a heavy-based saucepan. Heat gently, stirring constantly, until melted. Pour into a bowl and leave to cool. Cover and chill for 1 hour, or until spreadable.

3 For the cake, place the butter and sugar in a bowl and beat together until light and fluffy. Gradually beat in the eggs. Stir in the golden syrup and ground almonds.

4 Sift the flour, salt and cocoa powder into a separate bowl, then fold into the mixture. Add a little water, if necessary, to make a dropping consistency. Spoon the mixture into the prepared tins and bake in the preheated oven for 30–35 minutes, or until springy to the touch and a skewer inserted in the centre comes out clean.

5 Cool in the tins for 5 minutes, then turn out onto a wire rack to cool completely.

6 When the cakes are cold, sandwich them together with one third of the icing. Spread the remaining icing over the top and sides of the cake, swirling it to give a frosted appearance.

7 Cut into slices and serve.

CAKES

CHOCOLATE ORANGE RING CAKE

Serves: 8–10

Prep: 40 mins, plus cooling

Cook: 45 mins

Ingredients

2 small oranges

85 g/3 oz plain chocolate

250 g/9 oz self-raising flour

1½ tsp baking powder

175 g/6 oz butter, softened, plus extra for greasing

200 g/7 oz caster sugar

3 eggs, beaten

Topping

175 g/6 oz icing sugar

2 tbsp orange juice

55 g/2 oz plain chocolate, broken into pieces

Method

1 Preheat the oven to 160°C/325°F/Gas Mark 3. Grease an 850-ml/1½-pint ring mould. Grate the rind from one of the oranges and set aside. Pare the rind from the other orange and set aside. Cut the skin and pith from the oranges, then cut them into segments by cutting down between the membranes with a sharp knife. Chop the segments into small pieces, reserving as much juice as possible. Grate the chocolate coarsely.

2 Sift the flour and baking powder into a bowl. Add the butter, caster sugar, eggs, grated orange rind and any reserved juice. Beat until the mixture is smooth. Fold in the chopped oranges and grated chocolate. Spoon the mixture into the prepared tin and bake in the preheated oven for 40 minutes, or until well risen and golden brown. Leave in the tin for 5 minutes, then turn out onto a wire rack to cool.

3 For the topping, sift the icing sugar into a bowl and stir in enough orange juice to make a coating consistency. Drizzle the icing over the cake. Put the chocolate in a heatproof bowl set over a saucepan of gently simmering water until melted. Drizzle the melted chocolate over the cake. Cut the reserved pared orange rind into thin strips and scatter over the cake.

CAKES

CHOCOLATE BROWNIE ROULADE

Serves: 6

Prep: 40 mins,
plus cooling & chilling

Cook: 30 mins

Ingredients

butter, for greasing

150 g/5½ oz plain chocolate, broken into pieces

3 tbsp water

175 g/6 oz caster sugar

5 eggs, separated

25 g/1 oz raisins, chopped

25 g/1 oz pecan nuts, chopped

pinch of salt

icing sugar, for dusting

300 ml/10 fl oz double cream, lightly whipped

Method

1 Preheat the oven to 180°C/350°F/Gas Mark 4. Grease a 30 x 20-cm/12 x 8-inch Swiss roll tin and line with baking paper. Melt the chocolate with the water in a small saucepan over a low heat until the chocolate has melted. Leave to cool. In a bowl, whisk the caster sugar and egg yolks for 2–3 minutes with an electric hand-held whisk until thick and pale. Fold in the cooled chocolate, raisins and pecan nuts. In a separate bowl, whisk the egg whites with the salt. Fold one quarter of the egg whites into the chocolate mixture, then fold in the rest of the whites, working lightly and quickly.

2 Transfer the mixture to the prepared tin and bake in the oven for 25 minutes, until risen and just firm to the touch. Leave to cool before covering with a sheet of baking paper and a damp clean tea towel. Leave until cold.

3 Turn the roulade out onto another piece of baking paper dusted with icing sugar and carefully remove the lining paper. Spread the cream over the roulade. Starting from a short end, roll the sponge away from you using the paper to guide you. Trim the ends of the roulade to make a neat finish and transfer to a serving plate. Chill in the refrigerator. Dust with icing sugar before serving.

CAKES

CHOCOLATE PETIT FOURS

Makes: 18

Prep: 40 mins,
plus chilling & cooling

Cook: 30 mins

Ingredients

4 eggs
50 g/1¾ oz caster sugar
85 g/3 oz plain flour
25 g/1 oz cocoa powder
20 g/¾ oz cornflour
200 g/7 oz cherry jam
3 tbsp kirsch

Icing

100 ml/3½ fl oz whipping cream
85 g/3 oz icing sugar
40 g/1½ oz butter
150 g/5½ oz plain chocolate, at least 70 percent cocoa solids, broken into pieces
18 sour cherries or maraschino cherries, to decorate

Method

1 Preheat the oven to 180°C/350°F/Gas Mark 4. Lir a baking tray with baking paper. Put the eggs and sugar into a large bowl and beat with an electric whisk until light and fluffy. Mix together th flour, cocoa powder and cornflour in a separate bowl, then fold into the egg mixture.

2 Spread the mixture evenly on the prepared baking tray and bake in the oven for 20 minutes. Remove from the oven, then lay a clean tea towel over the cake and quickly invert. Remove the baking tray and carefully peel off the baking paper.

3 Heat the jam in a small saucepan and stir in the kirsch. Cut the chocolate cake in half horizontall On one half, spread the prepared jam evenly over the entire surface. Stack the remaining half on top. Chill in the refrigerator for 30 minutes.

4 To make the icing, heat the cream in a saucepa with the icing sugar. Stir in the butter, then add th chocolate piece by piece. Remove from the he and leave to cool until thick, but still liquid.

5 Meanwhile, cut the chilled cake into 18 pieces and transfer to a wire rack set over a sheet of baking paper. Pour the icing over the cakes, the place a sour cherry on each petit four.

CAKES

VICTORIA SPONGE CAKE

Serves: 8   **Prep: 25 mins,**   **Cook: 25–30 mins**
plus cooling

Ingredients

175 g/6 oz self-raising flour

1 tsp baking powder

175 g/6 oz butter, softened, plus extra for greasing

175 g/6 oz golden caster sugar

3 eggs

icing sugar, for dusting

Filling

3 tbsp raspberry jam

300 ml/10 fl oz double cream, whipped

16 fresh strawberries, halved

Method

1 Preheat the oven to 180°C/350°F/Gas Mark 4. Grease two 20-cm/8-inch sandwich tins and line with baking paper.

2 Sift the flour and baking powder into a bowl and add the butter, sugar and eggs. Mix together, then beat well until smooth.

3 Divide the mixture evenly between the prepared tins and smooth the surfaces. Bake in the preheated oven for 25–30 minutes, or until well risen and golden brown, and the cakes feel springy when lightly pressed.

4 Leave to cool in the tins for 5 minutes, then turn out and peel off the baking paper. Transfer to wire racks to cool completely. Sandwich the cakes together with the raspberry jam, whipped double cream and strawberry halves. Dust with icing sugar.

CAKES

LEMON DRIZZLE LOAF

Serves: 8–10 **Prep: 25 mins,** plus cooling **Cook: 45–55 mins**

Ingredients

oil or melted butter, for greasing

175 g/6 oz plain flour

1 tbsp baking powder

175 g/6 oz unsalted butter, softened

175 g/6 oz golden caster sugar

3 eggs, beaten

1 egg yolk

finely grated rind of 1 lemon

2 tbsp lemon juice

fine strips of lemon zest, to decorate

Syrup

85 g/3 oz icing sugar

3 tbsp lemon juice

Method

1 Preheat the oven to 180°C/350°F/Gas Mark 4. Grease and line a 1.2-litre/2-pint loaf tin.

2 Sift the flour and baking powder into a large bowl and add the butter, caster sugar, eggs and egg yolk. Beat well until the mixture is smooth, then stir in the lemon rind and juice.

3 Spoon the mixture into the prepared tin and smooth the surface with a palette knife. Bake in the preheated oven for 40–50 minutes, or until well risen, firm and golden brown.

4 Remove the tin from the oven and transfer to a wire rack. For the syrup, place the icing sugar and lemon juice in a saucepan and heat gently without boiling, stirring until the sugar dissolves.

5 Prick the top of the loaf several times with a skewer and spoon over the syrup. Leave to cool completely in the tin, then turn out, scatter with strips of lemon zest and cut into slices.

CAKES

FROSTED CARROT CAKE

Serves: 16

Prep: 35 mins,
plus cooling

Cook: 40–45 mins

Ingredients

175 ml/6 fl oz sunflower oil, plus extra for greasing

175 g/6 oz light muscovado sugar

3 eggs, beaten

175 g/6 oz grated carrots

85 g/3 oz sultanas

55 g/2 oz walnut pieces

grated rind of 1 orange

175 g/6 oz self-raising flour

1 tsp bicarbonate of soda

1 tsp ground cinnamon

½ tsp grated nutmeg

strips of orange zest, to decorate

Frosting

200 g/7 oz cream cheese

100 g/3½ oz icing sugar

2 tsp orange juice

Method

1 Preheat the oven to 180°C/350°F/Gas Mark 4. Grease and line a 23-cm/9-inch square cake tin.

2 In a large bowl beat together the oil, sugar and eggs. Stir in the grated carrots, sultanas, walnut pieces and orange rind.

3 Sift the flour, bicarbonate of soda, cinnamon and nutmeg together into the bowl, then mix evenly into the carrot mixture.

4 Spoon the mixture into the prepared cake tin and bake in the preheated oven for 40–45 minutes, until well risen and firm to the touch.

5 Cool in the tin for 5 minutes, then turn out onto a wire rack to cool completely.

6 For the frosting, combine the cream cheese, icing sugar and orange juice in a bowl and beat until smooth. Spread over the top of the cake and swirl with a palette knife.

7 Decorate with strips of orange zest, cut into squares and serve.

LEMON & BLUEBERRY POLENTA CAKE

Serves: 8　　　　**Prep: 20 mins,** plus cooling　　　　**Cook: 40–45 mins**

Ingredients

125 g/4½ oz butter, softened, plus extra for greasing

150 g/5½ oz caster sugar

finely grated rind of 1 lemon, plus 2 tbsp juice

3 eggs, beaten

115 g/4 oz polenta

115 g/4 oz ground almonds

1 tsp baking powder

4 tbsp Greek-style yogurt

115 g/4 oz fresh or frozen blueberries

icing sugar, for dusting

Method

1 Preheat the oven to 180°C/350°F/Gas Mark 4. Grease a 20-cm/8-inch round springform cake tin and line with baking paper.

2 Put the butter, caster sugar, lemon rind and lemon juice into a large bowl and beat together until pale and fluffy. Gradually beat in the eggs, then stir in the polenta, ground almonds, baking powder and yogurt.

3 Fold in two thirds of the blueberries. Spoon the mixture into the prepared tin, smooth the surface and scatter over the remaining blueberries.

4 Bake in the preheated oven for 40–45 minutes, or until just firm and deep golden around the edges. Leave to cool in the tin for 20 minutes, then unclip the tin and carefully transfer the cake to a wire rack. Serve warm or cold, dusted with icing sugar.

CAKES

BLUEBERRY CRUMB CAKE

Serves: 10   **Prep: 25 mins,**   **Cook: 1–1¼ hours**
                     plus cooling

Ingredients

175 g/6 oz butter, softened,
plus extra for greasing

175 g/6 oz caster sugar

3 large eggs, beaten

4 tbsp buttermilk

200 g/7 oz self-raising flour

55 g/2 oz ground almonds

175 g/6 oz blueberries

Crumb topping

85 g/3 oz self-raising flour

55 g/2 oz butter,
chilled and diced

55 g/2 oz demerara sugar

55 g/2 oz chopped
mixed nuts

Method

1 Preheat the oven to 180°C/350°F/Gas Mark 4.
   Grease and line a 23-cm/9-inch round
   springform cake tin.

2 Place the butter and caster sugar in a large
   bowl and beat together until pale and fluffy,
   then gradually beat in the eggs. Stir in the
   buttermilk. Sift over the flour and fold in gently
   until thoroughly incorporated. Fold in the
   ground almonds.

3 Spread half the mixture into the prepared tin
   and scatter over half the blueberries. Spoon over
   the remaining mixture and spread evenly. Top
   with the rest of the blueberries.

4 For the crumb topping, sift the flour into a bowl,
   then add the butter and rub in until the mixture
   resembles breadcrumbs. Stir in the demerara
   sugar and nuts. Sprinkle the mixture evenly over
   the cake.

5 Bake in the preheated oven for 1–1¼ hours, or
   until golden brown and firm to the touch. Leave
   to cool in the tin for 20 minutes then unclip the
   tin and transfer to a wire rack to cool completely.
   Slice to serve.

RICH FRUIT CAKE

Serves: 16

Prep: 35 mins, plus soaking, cooling & storing

Cook: 2¼–2¾ hours

Ingredients

350 g/12 oz sultanas

225 g/8 oz raisins

115 g/4 oz ready-to-eat dried apricots, chopped

85 g/3 oz stoned dates, chopped

4 tbsp dark rum or brandy, plus extra for flavouring (optional)

finely grated rind and juice of 1 orange

225 g/8 oz unsalted butter, softened, plus extra for greasing

225 g/8 oz light muscovado sugar

4 eggs, beaten

70 g/2½ oz chopped mixed peel

85 g/3 oz glacé cherries, quartered

25 g/1 oz chopped glacé ginger or stem ginger

40 g/1½ oz blanched almonds, chopped

200 g/7 oz plain flour

1 tsp ground mixed spice

Method

1 Place the sultanas, raisins, apricots and dates in a large bowl and stir in the rum, if using, orange rind and orange juice. Cover and leave to soak for several hours or overnight. Preheat the oven to 150°C/300°F/Gas Mark 2. Grease a 20-cm/ 8-inch round cake tin and line with baking paper.

2 Beat the butter and sugar together until pale and creamy. Gradually beat in the eggs, beating hard after each addition. Stir in the soaked fruits, mixed peel, glacé cherries, glacé ginger and blanched almonds. Sift the flour and mixed spice, then fold lightly and evenly into the mixture. Spoon the mixture into the prepared cake tin and smooth the surface, making a slight depression in the centre with the back of the spoon.

3 Bake in the preheated oven for 2¼–2¾ hours, or until the cake is beginning to shrink away from the sides and a skewer inserted into the centre comes out clean. Cool completely in the tin.

4 Turn out the cake and remove the baking paper. Wrap in some greaseproof paper and foil, and store for at least two months before use. To add a richer flavour, prick the cake with a skewer and spoon over a couple of extra tablespoons of rum or brandy, if using, before storing.

CAKES

COFFEE & WALNUT CAKE

Serves: 8

Prep: 35 mins, plus cooling

Cook: 20–25 mins

Ingredients

175 g/6 oz unsalted butter, softened, plus extra for greasing

175 g/6 oz light muscovado sugar

3 large eggs, beaten

175 g/6 oz self-raising flour

1½ tsp baking powder

115 g/4 oz walnut pieces

3 tbsp strong black coffee

walnut halves, to decorate

Frosting

115 g/4 oz unsalted butter, softened

200 g/7 oz icing sugar

1 tbsp strong black coffee

½ tsp vanilla extract

Method

1 Preheat the oven to 180°C/350°F/Gas Mark 4. Grease two 20-cm/8-inch sandwich tins and line with baking paper.

2 Beat the butter and muscovado sugar together until pale and creamy. Gradually add the eggs, beating well after each addition.

3 Sift the flour and baking powder into the mixture, then fold in lightly and evenly with a metal spoon. Fold in the walnut pieces and the coffee. Divide the mixture between the prepared cake tins and smooth the surfaces. Bake in the preheated oven for 20–25 minutes, or until golden brown and springy to the touch. Turn out onto a wire rack to cool completely.

4 To make the frosting, beat together the butter, icing sugar, coffee and vanilla extract, mixing until smooth and creamy.

5 Use about half the mixture to sandwich the cakes together, then spread the remaining frosting on top and swirl with a palette knife. Decorate with walnut halves.

CAKES

DATE & WALNUT LOAF

Serves: 8

Prep: 25 mins,
plus soaking & cooling

Cook: 35–40 mins

Ingredients

100 g/3½ oz dates, stoned and chopped

½ tsp bicarbonate of soda

finely grated rind of ½ lemon

100 ml/3½ fl oz hot tea

40 g/1½ oz unsalted butter, plus extra for greasing

70 g/2½ oz light muscovado sugar

1 small egg

125 g/4½ oz self-raising flour

25 g/1 oz walnuts, chopped

walnut halves, to decorate

Method

1 Preheat the oven to 180°C/350°F/Gas Mark 4. Grease a 450-g/1-lb loaf tin and line with baking paper.

2 Place the dates, bicarbonate of soda and lemon rind in a bowl and add the hot tea. Leave to soak for 10 minutes until softened.

3 Cream the butter and sugar together until light and fluffy, then beat in the egg. Stir in the date mixture.

4 Fold in the flour using a large metal spoon, then fold in the walnuts. Spoon the mixture into the prepared cake tin and smooth the surface. Top with the walnut halves.

5 Bake in the preheated oven for 35–40 minutes or until risen, firm and golden brown. Cool for 10 minutes in the tin, then turn out onto a wire rack to cool completely.

CAKES

CHERRY CAKE

Makes: 20

Prep: 30 mins, plus cooling

Cook: 1 hour

Ingredients

2 tbsp dried breadcrumbs

500 g/1 lb 2 oz cherries

150 g/5½ oz softened butter, plus extra for greasing

150 g/5½ oz caster sugar

4 eggs, separated

70 g/2½ oz ground almonds

150 g/5½ oz plain flour

½ tsp baking powder

icing sugar, for dusting

Method

1 Preheat the oven to 180°C/350°F/Gas Mark 4. Grease a 20 x 30-cm/8 x 12-inch rectangular cake tin and sprinkle with the breadcrumbs. Stone the cherries.

2 Put the butter and sugar into a large bowl and beat with an electric mixer until fluffy. Add the egg yolks, one at a time, beating after each addition until combined. Whisk the egg whites until they hold stiff peaks. Stir the almonds, flour and baking powder into the butter mixture, then fold in the beaten egg whites.

3 Spoon the mixture into the prepared tin and scatter the cherries on top.

4 Bake on the bottom shelf of the preheated oven for 50 minutes. At the end of the cooking time, switch off the oven and leave the cake inside for a further 10 minutes.

5 Remove from the oven and leave to cool in the tin. Turn out of the tin, dust with icing sugar, cut into squares and serve.

CAKES

STICKY GINGER LOAF

Serves: 8–10

Prep: 25 mins,
plus cooling

Cook: 1–1¼ hours

Ingredients

oil or melted butter,
for greasing

75 g/6 oz plain white flour

1 tbsp baking powder

1 tbsp ground ginger

175 ml/6 fl oz sunflower oil

5 g/3 oz dark muscovado
sugar

85 g/3 oz golden syrup

3 eggs, beaten

3 pieces stem ginger in
syrup, drained and finely
chopped, plus 2 tbsp syrup
from the jar

sliced stem ginger,
to decorate

Method

1 Preheat the oven to 180°C/350°F/Gas Mark 4.
Grease and line a 1.2-litre/2-pint loaf tin.

2 Sift the flour, baking powder and ground ginger
into a large bowl. Add the oil, sugar, golden syrup
and eggs, then beat well to a smooth batter. Stir
in the chopped ginger.

3 Pour the mixture into the prepared tin. Bake in
the preheated oven for 1–1¼ hours, until well
risen and firm.

4 Leave to cool in the tin for 10 minutes, then turn
out and finish cooling on a wire rack. To serve,
brush the top of the cake with the ginger syrup,
decorate with sliced ginger and cut into slices.

CAKES

PEAR & BLACKBERRY CAKE

Serves: 16

Prep: 40 mins,
plus rising & cooling

Cook: 40 mins

Ingredients

500 g/1 lb 2 oz plain flour,
plus extra for dusting

50 g/1¾ oz caster sugar

pinch of salt

3 tsp easy-blend dried
yeast (1½ x 7-g sachets)

125 g/4½ oz butter,
plus extra for greasing

280 ml/9½ fl oz
lukewarm milk

Topping

3 pears

pared rind of 1 orange

250 g/9 oz blackberries

50 g/1¾ oz soft light
brown sugar

100 g/3½ oz quince jelly

icing sugar, for dusting

Method

1 To make the cake, sift the flour, sugar and salt
into a large bowl then stir in the yeast. Make a
well in the centre.

2 Melt the butter in a saucepan over a low heat,
then add to the dry ingredients with the milk,
mixing to a soft, smooth dough. Cover with a
damp tea towel and leave to rise in a warm
place for about 30 minutes, or until risen and
springy to the touch.

3 To make the topping, peel, quarter and core the
pears, then cut the quarters into slices. Cut the
orange rind into narrow strips.

4 Grease a 30 x 40-cm/12 x16-inch baking tray.
Roll out the dough, on a work surface lightly
dusted with flour, to a rectangle the size of the
prepared tray. Lay the dough in the tray. Arrange
the pears, blackberries and strips of orange rind
evenly on top, pressing them into the dough
slightly, then sprinkle over the brown sugar. Leave
to rise for 30 minutes.

5 Meanwhile, preheat the oven to 200°C/400°F/
Gas Mark 6. Bake the cake in the preheated
oven for about 30 minutes. Put the quince jelly
into a small saucepan and heat over a low heat.
Brush the jelly on the warm cake and leave to
cool. Dust with icing sugar just before serving.

CAKES

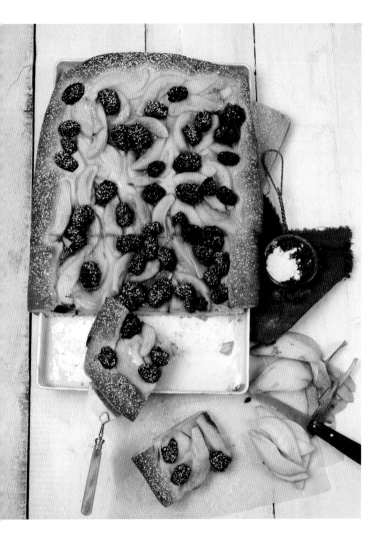

FRUIT & NUT LOAF

Serves: 8–10

Prep: 30 mins,
plus cooling

Cook: 1–1¼ hours

Ingredients

175 g/6 oz butter, softened, plus extra for greasing

115 g/4 oz light muscovado sugar

2 tbsp set honey

3 eggs, beaten

200 g/7 oz wholemeal self-raising flour

½ tsp baking powder

115 g/4 oz sultanas

85 g/3 oz ready-to-eat dried apricots, chopped

85 g/3 oz glacé cherries, quartered

25 g/1 oz walnuts, roughly chopped

25 g/1 oz macadamia nuts, roughly chopped

Buttercream

85 g/3 oz unsalted butter, softened

2 tsp finely grated orange rind

1 tbsp orange juice

175 g/6 oz icing sugar

Method

1 Preheat the oven to 160°C/325°F/Gas Mark 3. Grease and line a 900-g/2-lb loaf tin.

2 Place the butter, sugar and honey in a large bowl and beat together until very pale and fluffy. Gradually beat in the eggs.

3 Sift the flour and baking powder into the mixture tipping any bran left in the sieve into the bowl. Fold in gently until thoroughly incorporated. Fold in the fruit and nuts.

4 Spoon the mixture into the prepared tin and gently smooth the surface. Bake in the preheated oven for 45 minutes then cover the top loosely with foil. Bake for a further 20–30 minutes, or until golden brown and a skewer inserted into the centre comes out clean. Cool in the tin for 15 minutes, then turn out onto a wire rack to cool completely.

5 For the buttercream, place the butter, orange rind and juice in a bowl and beat together until smooth. Gradually beat in the icing sugar. Spread over the top of the cake. Cut into slices to serve.

APPLE & SPICE CAKE

Serves: 8

Prep: 30 mins, plus standing & optional cooling

Cook: 50–60 mins

Ingredients

175 g/6 oz butter, softened, plus extra for greasing

175 g/6 oz caster sugar

finely grated zest of 1 lemon

2 large eggs, beaten

175 g/6 oz self-raising flour

4 tbsp milk

Topping

55 g/2 oz demerara sugar

1 tsp ground cinnamon

¼ tsp ground cloves

2 crisp dessert apples, such as Granny Smith or Pink Lady

25 g/1 oz butter, melted and cooled

whipped cream or vanilla ice cream, to serve

Method

1 Preheat the oven to 180°C/350°F/Gas Mark 4. Lightly grease a 20-cm/8-inch springform cake tin and line the base with non-stick baking paper. Beat the butter, sugar and lemon zest together until pale and creamy. Gradually add the eggs, beating well between each addition.

2 Fold in half the flour and milk using a large metal spoon, then fold in the remainder until the mixture is smooth. Spoon into the prepared tin and level the surface.

3 To make the topping, mix the sugar, cinnamon and cloves together and sprinkle half the mixture over the cake. Peel, core and thinly slice the apples then spread them evenly on top. Sprinkle with the remaining sugar mixture. Drizzle the melted butter over the top.

4 Bake in the preheated oven for 50–60 minutes until golden brown and the centre is firm to the touch. Leave to stand for 10 minutes, then turn out and remove the lining paper. Serve warm with whipped cream, or leave to cool and cut into slices.

APPLE STREUSEL CAKE

Serves: 8 **Prep: 40 mins,** **Cook: 1 hour**
plus cooling

Ingredients

450 g/1 lb cooking apples
175 g/6 oz self-raising flour
1 tsp ground cinnamon
pinch of salt
115 g/4 oz butter,
plus extra for greasing
115 g/4 oz caster sugar
2 eggs
1–2 tbsp milk
icing sugar, for dusting

Streusel topping

115 g/4 oz self-raising flour
85 g/3 oz butter
85 g/3 oz caster sugar

Method

1 Preheat the oven to 180°C/350°F/Gas Mark 4,
then grease a 23-cm/9-inch springform cake tin.
To make the streusel topping, sift the flour into
a bowl and rub in the butter until the mixture
resembles coarse crumbs. Stir in the sugar
and reserve.

2 To make the cake, peel, core and thinly slice
the apples. Sift the flour into a bowl with the
cinnamon and salt. Place the butter and sugar
in a separate bowl and beat together until light
and fluffy. Gradually beat in the eggs, adding
a little of the flour mixture with the last addition
of egg. Gently fold in half the remaining flour
mixture, then fold in the rest with the milk.

3 Spoon the mixture into the prepared tin and
smooth the top. Cover with the sliced apples
and sprinkle the streusel topping evenly over
the top.

4 Bake in the preheated oven for 1 hour, or until
browned and firm to the touch. Leave to cool in
the tin before opening the sides. Dust the cake
with icing sugar before serving.

CITRUS MOUSSE CAKE

Serves: 8

Prep: 40 mins,
plus cooling, setting &
chilling

Cook: 50 mins

Ingredients

175 g/6 oz butter,
plus extra for greasing

175 g/6 oz caster sugar

4 eggs, lightly beaten

200 g/7 oz self-raising flour

1 tbsp cocoa powder

50 g/1¾ oz orange-
flavoured plain
chocolate, melted

peeled orange segments,
to decorate

Orange Mousse

2 eggs, separated

50 g/1¾ oz caster sugar

200 ml/7 fl oz freshly
squeezed orange juice

2 tsp gelatine

3 tbsp water

300 ml/10 fl oz double
cream

Method

1 Preheat the oven to 180°C/350°F/Gas Mark 4.
Grease and line the base of a 20-cm/8-inch
round springform cake tin.

2 Beat the butter and sugar in a bowl until light
and fluffy. Gradually add the eggs, beating well
after each addition. Sift together the flour and
cocoa and fold into the creamed mixture. Fold
in the melted chocolate.

3 Pour into the prepared tin and level the top.
Bake in the preheated oven for 40 minutes,
or until springy to the touch. Leave to cool for
5 minutes in the tin, then turn out onto a wire
rack and leave to cool completely. Cut the
cold cake horizontally into 2 layers.

4 To make the orange mousse, beat the egg yolks
and sugar until pale, then whisk in the orange
juice. Sprinkle the gelatine over the water in a
small heatproof bowl and allow to go spongy,
then place over a saucepan of hot water and
stir until dissolved. Stir into the egg yolk mixture.
Whip the cream until holding its shape, reserve
a little for decoration, then fold the remainder
into the orange mixture. Whisk the egg whites
until standing in soft peaks, then fold in. Leave
in a cool place until starting to set, stirring
occasionally.

CAKES

5 Place half of the cake back in the tin. Pour in the mousse and press the second cake layer on top. Chill until set. Transfer to a serving plate, spoon teaspoonfuls of cream around the top and decorate the centre with orange segments.

PINEAPPLE & COCONUT BUNDT CAKE

Serves: 12

Prep: 30 mins, plus cooling

Cook: 25 mins

Ingredients

432 g/15½ oz canned pineapple rings, drained

115 g/4 oz unsalted butter, softened, plus extra for greasing

175 g/6 oz caster sugar

2 eggs and 1 egg yolk, beaten together

225 g/8 oz plain flour

1 tsp baking powder

½ tsp bicarbonate of soda

40 g/1½ oz desiccated coconut

Frosting

175 g/6 oz cream cheese

175 g/6 oz icing sugar

Method

1 Preheat the oven to 180°C/350°F/Gas Mark 4. Grease a 24-cm/9½-inch ring mould.

2 Place the pineapple rings in a blender or food processor and process briefly until just crushed.

3 Beat together the butter and caster sugar until light and fluffy.

4 Gradually beat in the eggs until combined.

5 Sift together the flour, baking powder and bicarbonate of soda over the egg mixture and fold in. Fold in the crushed pineapple and the coconut.

6 Spoon the mixture into the prepared tin and bake in the preheated oven for 25 minutes until a skewer inserted into the centre comes out clean.

7 Leave to cool in the tin for 10 minutes before turning out onto a wire rack to cool completely.

8 To make the frosting, mix together the cream cheese and icing sugar and spread over the cooled cake.

9 Cut into slices and serve immediately.

CAKES

HONEY & ALMOND CAKE

Serves: 8–10 approx   **Prep: 20 mins,** plus cooling   **Cook: 40–45 mins**

Ingredients

150 g/5½ oz unsalted butter, plus extra for greasing

115 g/4 oz light muscovado sugar

175 g/6 oz clear honey

1 tbsp lemon juice

2 eggs, beaten

200 g/7 oz self-raising flour

15 g/½ oz flaked almonds

warmed honey, to glaze

Method

1 Preheat the oven to 180°C/350°F/Gas Mark 4. Grease and line a 20-cm/8-inch deep cake tin.

2 Place the butter, sugar, honey and lemon juice in a saucepan and stir over a medium heat, without boiling, until melted and smooth.

3 Remove the pan from the heat and quickly beat in the eggs with a wooden spoon. Sift in the flour and stir lightly with a metal spoon. Pour into the prepared tin and scatter the almonds over the top.

4 Bake in the preheated oven for 35–40 minutes, until risen, firm and golden brown. Cool in the tin for 15 minutes, then turn out onto a wire rack to cool completely.

5 Brush with the warmed honey and cut into slices to serve.

COCONUT CAKE

Serves: 6–8

Prep: 20 mins, plus cooling

Cook: 1 hour

Ingredients

225 g/8 oz self-raising flour

pinch of salt

115 g/4 oz butter, cut into small pieces, plus extra for greasing

115 g/4 oz demerara sugar

100 g/3½ oz grated coconut, plus extra for sprinkling

2 eggs, lightly beaten

4 tbsp milk

Method

1 Preheat the oven to 160°C/325°F/Gas Mark 3. Grease a 900-g/2-lb loaf tin and line with baking paper.

2 Sift the flour and salt into a mixing bowl and rub in the butter with your fingertips until the mixture resembles fine breadcrumbs. Stir in the sugar, coconut, eggs and milk and mix to a soft dropping consistency.

3 Spoon the mixture into the prepared tin and smooth the surface with a palette knife. Bake in the preheated oven for 30 minutes.

4 Remove the cake from the oven and sprinkle with the extra coconut. Return the cake to the oven and bake for an additional 30 minutes, until well risen and golden and a skewer inserted into the centre comes out clean.

5 Leave the cake to cool slightly in the tin, then turn out onto a wire rack to cool completely.

CAKES

STRAWBERRY SHORTCAKE

Serves: 6–8

Prep: 30 mins,
plus cooling

Cook: 15–20 mins

Ingredients

250 g/9 oz self-raising flour

50 g/1¾ oz butter, diced,
plus extra for greasing

50 g/1¾ oz caster sugar

125–150 ml/4–5 fl oz milk

fresh mint leaves, to garnish

Topping

4 tbsp milk

250 g/1 lb 2 oz mascarpone
cheese

5 tbsp caster sugar

500 g/1 lb 2 oz strawberries,
hulled and quartered

finely grated rind of
1 orange

Method

1 Preheat the oven to 200°C/400°F/Gas Mark 6.
Lightly grease a 20-cm/8-inch loose-based
cake tin.

2 To make the base, sift the flour into a large bowl,
add the butter and rub in with your fingertips
until the mixture resembles fine breadcrumbs.
Add the caster sugar. Stir in enough of the milk to
form a soft but smooth dough. Gently press the
dough evenly into the prepared cake tin. Bake in
the preheated oven for 15–20 minutes until risen,
firm to the touch and golden brown. Leave to
cool for 5 minutes in the tin, then turn out onto a
wire rack and leave to cool completely.

3 To make the topping, beat together the milk
and mascarpone cheese with 3 tablespoons
of the caster sugar in a bowl until smooth and
fluffy. Put the strawberries in a separate bowl
and sprinkle with the remaining caster sugar
and the orange rind.

4 Spread the mascarpone mixture over the scone
base and pile the strawberries on top. Spoon
over any juices left over from the strawberries in
the bowl, scatter with mint leaves and serve.

CAKES

RASPBERRY CHARLOTTE

Serves: 8–10

Prep: 40 mins,
plus soaking, chilling &
setting

Cook: 5–10 mins

Ingredients

800 g/1 lb 12 oz fresh
raspberries, plus extra
to decorate

9 gelatine leaves

175 g/6 oz caster sugar

3–4 tbsp water, plus extra
for soaking

grated rind of ½ unwaxed
lemon

25–30 sponge fingers

400 ml/14 fl oz whipping
cream

icing sugar, to decorate

whipped cream, to serve
(optional)

Method

1 Purée the raspberries in a food processor, then pass them through a sieve to remove the seeds. Soak the gelatine in a bowl of cold water. Heat the sugar in a small saucepan with the water, stirring until the sugar crystals have dissolved. Remove the sugar syrup from the stove, squeeze the excess water out of the soaked gelatine, add to the syrup and stir to dissolve. Stir in the raspberry purée and lemon rind. Cover and chill in the refrigerator until the mixture begins to set.

2 Place a 26-cm/10½-inch cake ring on a plate. Cover the plate completely with tightly packed sponge fingers. Completely line the ring with sponge fingers arranged vertically, leaving no gaps.

3 Whip the cream until it holds stiff peaks, then fold it into the raspberry mixture. Carefully fill the cake ring with the raspberry mixture, making sure that the sponges do not slip out of place, then smooth the top. Leave to set slightly.

4 Carefully remove the cake ring. Decorate with raspberries and dust with icing sugar. Serve chilled, with dollops of whipped cream, if liked.

FRUITS OF THE FOREST CHEESECAKE

Serves: 8-10

Prep: 35 mins,
plus chilling & soaking

Cook: 10 mins

Ingredients

250 g/9 oz digestive biscuits

120 g/4¼ oz butter

85 g/3 oz caster sugar

pinch of ground cinnamon

Topping

3 egg yolks

100 g/3½ oz caster sugar

500 g/1 lb 2 oz mascarpone cheese

500 g/1 lb 2 oz mixed berries, such as raspberries, blackberries and blueberries

12 sheets leaf gelatine

250 ml/9 fl oz whipping cream

85 g/3 oz sweet square biscuits

icing sugar, for dusting

Method

1 To make the base, put the biscuits into a polythene bag and crush with a rolling pin until reduced to fine crumbs. Melt the butter in a saucepan, add the biscuit crumbs, sugar and cinnamon and mix to combine. Line the base of a 24-cm/9½-inch round springform tin with baking paper, press the biscuit mixture into the base, then chill in the refrigerator for 30 minutes.

2 To make the topping, put the egg yolks into a large bowl with the sugar and beat with an electric mixer until fluffy. Add the mascarpone cheese and 300 g/10½ oz of the berries. Soak the gelatine in cold water for 10 minutes, then squeeze out the water. Put the gelatine into a saucepan with a little water and heat over a low heat, stirring constantly, until dissolved. Stir the gelatine into the mascarpone mixture.

3 Whip the cream until it holds stiff peaks and fold it into the mascarpone mixture. Spread the mixture on the base, cover with clingfilm and chill in the refrigerator for 4 hours.

4 Remove the cake from the refrigerator and decorate with the remaining berries. Unclip and release the springform, arrange the biscuits around the edge of the cake and dust with icing sugar.

NEW YORK CHEESECAKE

Serves: 10

Prep: 35 mins,
plus cooling & chilling

Cook: 1 hour
(plus cooling & setting
in turned off oven)

Ingredients

100 g/3½ oz butter,
plus extra for greasing

150 g/5½ oz digestive
biscuits, finely crushed

1 tbsp granulated sugar

900 g/2 lb cream cheese

250 g/9 oz caster sugar

2 tbsp plain flour

1 tsp vanilla extract

finely grated zest of
1 orange

finely grated zest of 1 lemon

3 eggs

2 egg yolks

300 ml/10 fl oz double
cream

Method

1 Preheat the oven to 180°C/350°F/Gas Mark 4.
Melt the butter in a small saucepan. Remove
from the heat and stir in the biscuit crumbs and
sugar. Press the biscuit mixture tightly into the
base of a 23-cm/9-inch round springform cake
tin. Place in the oven and bake for 10 minutes.
Remove from the oven and leave to cool.

2 Increase the oven temperature to 200°C/400°F/
Gas Mark 6. Use an electric mixer to beat the
cream cheese until creamy, then gradually add
the caster sugar and flour and beat until smooth.
Increase the speed and beat in the vanilla
extract, orange zest and lemon zest, then beat
in the eggs and egg yolks one at a time. Finally,
beat in the cream. It should be light and fluffy –
beat on a faster setting if you need to.

3 Grease the sides of the cake tin and pour in
the filling. Smooth the top, transfer to the oven
and bake for 15 minutes, then reduce the
temperature to 110°C/225°F/Gas Mark ¼ and
bake for a further 30 minutes. Turn off the oven
and leave the cheesecake in it for 2 hours to
cool and set. Chill in the refrigerator overnight
before serving. Slide a knife around the edge
of the cake then unclip and remove from the
tin to serve.

LEMON CHEESECAKE

Serves: 8

Prep: 25 mins,
plus chilling & cooling

Cook: 45–50 mins

Ingredients

55 g/2 oz butter,
plus extra for greasing

175 g/6 oz gingernut
biscuits, crushed

3 lemons

300 g/10½ oz ricotta
cheese

200 g/7 oz Greek-style
yogurt

4 eggs, beaten

1 tbsp cornflour

100 g/3½ oz caster sugar

strips of lemon zest,
to decorate

icing sugar, for dusting

Method

1. Preheat the oven to 180°C/350°F/Gas Mark 4. Grease a 20-cm/8-inch round springform cake tin and line with baking paper.

2. Melt the butter in a saucepan and stir in the biscuit crumbs. Press into the base of the prepared cake tin. Chill until firm.

3. Meanwhile, finely grate the rind from the lemons into a bowl and squeeze the juice. Add the ricotta, yogurt, eggs, cornflour and caster sugar and whisk until a smooth batter is formed.

4. Carefully spoon the mixture into the tin. Bake in the preheated oven for 40–45 minutes, or until just firm and golden brown.

5. Cool the cheesecake completely in the tin, then run a knife around the edge to loosen and turn out onto a serving plate. Decorate with lemon zest and dust with icing sugar.

★ **Variation**

Top your cheesecake with a delicious coulis by cooking 400 g/14 oz of fruit, such as blueberries, for 5 minutes with two tablespoons of water. Sieve the mixture, then stir in one tablespoon of sifted icing sugar. Leave to cool before serving.

DESSERTS

PEACH COBBLER

Serves: 6   **Prep: 30 mins**   **Cook: 35 mins**

Ingredients

Filling

6 peaches, peeled, stoned and sliced

4 tbsp caster sugar

½ tbsp lemon juice

1½ tsp cornflour

½ tsp almond extract or vanilla extract

ice cream, to serve

Topping

185 g/6½ oz plain flour

115 g/4 oz caster sugar

1½ tsp baking powder

½ tsp salt

85 g/3 oz butter, diced

1 egg

6 tbsp milk

Method

1 Preheat the oven to 220°C/425°F/Gas Mark 7. Place the peaches in a 23-cm/9-inch square baking dish. Add the sugar, lemon juice, cornflour and almond extract and toss together. Bake in the preheated oven for 20 minutes.

2 Meanwhile, to make the topping, sift the flour, all but 2 tablespoons of the sugar, the baking powder and the salt into a bowl. Rub in the butter with your fingertips until the mixture resembles breadcrumbs. Mix the egg and 5 tablespoons of the milk in a jug, then mix into the dry ingredients with a fork until a soft, sticky dough forms. If the dough seems too dry, stir in the extra tablespoon of milk.

3 Reduce the oven temperature to 200°C/400°F/Gas Mark 6. Remove the peaches from the oven and drop spoonfuls of the topping over the surface, without smoothing. Sprinkle with the remaining sugar, return to the oven and bake for a further 15 minutes, or until the topping is golden brown and firm – the topping will spread as it cooks. Serve hot or at room temperature, with ice cream.

★ Variation

Instead of peaches, try halved apricots or halved plums.

DESSERTS

RHUBARB CRUMBLE

Serves: 6   **Prep: 25 mins**   **Cook: 25–30 mins**

Ingredients

900 g/2 lb rhubarb

115 g/4 oz caster sugar

grated rind and juice of
1 orange

cream, yogurt or custard,
to serve

Crumble topping

225 g/8 oz plain or
wholemeal flour

115 g/4 oz unsalted butter

115 g/4 oz soft brown sugar

1 tsp ground ginger

Method

1 Preheat the oven to 190°C/375°F/Gas Mark 5.

2 Cut the rhubarb into 2.5-cm/1-inch lengths and place in a 1.7-litre/3-pint ovenproof dish with the sugar and the orange rind and juice.

3 Make the crumble topping by placing the flour in a mixing bowl and rubbing in the unsalted butter until the mixture resembles breadcrumbs. Stir in the sugar and the ginger.

4 Spread the crumble evenly over the fruit and press down lightly using a fork. Bake in the centre of the oven on a baking tray for 25–30 minutes until the crumble is golden brown.

5 Serve warm with cream.

APPLE & BLACKBERRY CRUMBLE

Serves: 4 **Prep: 25 mins** **Cook: 40–45 mins**

Ingredients

900 g/2 lb cooking apples

300 g/10½ oz blackberries, fresh or frozen

55 g/2 oz light muscovado sugar

1 tsp ground cinnamon

custard or pouring cream, to serve (optional)

Crumble topping

85 g/3 oz self-raising flour

85 g/3 oz wholemeal plain flour

115 g/4 oz unsalted butter, diced

55 g/2 oz demerara sugar

Method

1 Preheat the oven to 200°C/400°F/Gas Mark 6. Peel and core the apples, then cut them into chunks. Put them in a bowl with the blackberries, muscovado sugar and cinnamon and mix together, then transfer to a 900-ml/1½-pint baking dish.

2 To make the crumble topping, sieve the self-raising flour into a bowl and stir in the wholemeal flour. Rub in the butter with your fingertips until the mixture resembles coarse breadcrumbs. Stir in the demerara sugar.

3 Spread the crumble topping over the fruit and bake in the preheated oven for 40–45 minutes, or until the apples are soft and the crumble is golden brown and crisp. Serve with custard, if using.

BLUEBERRY CRUMBLE WITH WALNUTS

Serves: 4

Prep: 30 mins, plus chilling

Cook: 35 mins

Ingredients

Base

250 g/9 oz plain flour, plus extra for dusting

1 tsp baking powder

75 g/2¾ oz caster sugar

1 tsp vanilla sugar

125 g/4½ oz butter, plus extra for greasing

2 eggs

2 tbsp dried breadcrumbs

Filling

400 g/14 oz blueberries

2 egg yolks

90 g/3¼ oz caster sugar

1 tbsp vanilla sugar

3 tbsp milk

100 g/3½ oz ground walnuts

120 g/4¼ oz plain flour

icing sugar, for dusting

Method

1 To make the base, mix together the flour, baking powder, caster sugar and vanilla sugar. Cut the butter into small pieces, rub into the flour mixture, then add the eggs. Quickly knead the mixture until a smooth dough forms. Wrap in clingfilm and chill in the refrigerator for at least 30 minutes.

2 Preheat the oven to 160°C/325°F/Gas Mark 3. Grease a 26-cm/10½-inch round tart tin.

3 Roll out the dough, on a work surface lightly dusted with flour, into a round slightly larger than the prepared tin. Use it to line the tin, turning up the edge of the dough. Prick the base several times with a fork and scatter over the breadcrumbs.

4 To make the filling, spread the blueberries over the base. Mix the egg yolks with the caster sugar, vanilla sugar and milk. Add the ground walnuts and flour and rub together with your fingertips until a crumbly texture is achieved. Scatter the crumble mixture over the blueberries.

5 Bake in the preheated oven for about 35 minutes until the crumble is light brown. Leave to cool slightly, then dust with icing sugar just before serving.

MERINGUE TORTE

Serves: 12

Prep: 40 mins,
plus chilling

Cook: 45 mins

Ingredients

300 g/10½ oz plain flour,
plus extra for dusting

2 tsp baking powder

140 g/5 oz caster sugar

140 g/5 oz butter,
room temperature,
plus extra for greasing

2 eggs, lightly beaten

Topping

3 egg yolks

1 egg

100 g/3½ oz caster sugar

1 tbsp lemon juice

300 ml/10 fl oz milk

500 g/1 lb 2 oz medium-fat
soft cheese or quark

150 g/5½ oz butter, melted

5 tbsp custard powder

Meringue

3 egg whites

4 tbsp caster sugar

250 g/9 oz redcurrants,
stems removed

icing sugar, for dusting

Method

1 Preheat the oven to 160°C/325°F/Gas Mark 3. Grease a 28-cm/11-inch baking tin, preferably springform, and line the base with baking paper.

2 To make the base, sift together the flour and baking powder in a bowl, add the sugar, butter and eggs. Mix using an electric mixer with a dough hook attachment, then briefly knead with your hands into a smooth mixture. Wrap in clingfilm and leave to rest in the refrigerator for 30 minutes.

3 Use floured hands to press and smooth the mixture evenly into the base of the tin.

4 To make the topping, mix together the egg yolks, egg, sugar and lemon juice in a bowl. Gradually stir in the milk, soft cheese, melted butter and custard powder until the mixture is smooth and has no lumps.

5 Pour the topping mixture over the torte base and smooth the surface. Bake in the preheated oven for about 30 minutes. Remove the cake, but leave the oven switched on.

6 To make the meringue, whisk the egg whites until almost stiff. Gradually whisk in the sugar. Continue whisking until the sugar is completely dissolved and the meringue holds stiff peaks.

7 Spread the meringue over the topping. Scatter the redcurrants over the top. Return the torte to the oven to bake for about 15 minutes. Leave to cool before removing from the tin. Dust with icing sugar before slicing and serving.

PEACH MELBA MERINGUE

Serves: 8

Prep: 45 mins,
plus cooling

Cook: 45–50 mins

Ingredients

Raspberry coulis

350 g/12 oz fresh raspberries
115 g/4 oz icing sugar

Meringue

2 tsp cornflour
300 g/10½ oz caster sugar
5 large egg whites
1 tsp cider vinegar

Filling

3 peaches, peeled, stoned
and chopped
250 g/9 oz fresh raspberries
200 ml/7 fl oz crème fraîche
150 ml/5 fl oz double cream

Method

1 Preheat the oven to 150°C/300°F/Gas Mark 2.
Line a 35 x 25-cm/14 x 10-inch Swiss roll tin with
nonstick baking paper. To make the coulis, purée
the raspberries and icing sugar together. Sieve
into a bowl and reserve.

2 To make the meringue, sift the cornflour and
sugar together. In a separate bowl, whisk the
egg whites into stiff peaks, then whisk in the
vinegar. Gradually whisk in the cornflour mixture
until stiff and glossy. Spread the mixture evenly
in the prepared tin, leaving a 1-cm/½-inch
border. Bake in the centre of the preheated
oven for 20 minutes, then reduce the heat to
110°C/225°F/Gas Mark ¼ and cook for a further
25–30 minutes, or until puffed up. Remove from
the oven. Leave to cool for 15 minutes. Turn out
onto a second piece of nonstick baking paper
and peel off the first.

3 To make the filling, mix the peaches and
raspberries in a bowl with 2 tablespoons of the
coulis. In a separate bowl, whisk together the
crème fraîche and cream until thick. Spread over
the meringue, then scatter over the fruit, leaving
a 3-cm/1¼-inch border at one short edge. Using
the baking paper, lift and roll the meringue from
the short edge without the border, ending up
seam-side down. Serve with the coulis.

DESSERTS

CHOCOLATE & RASPBERRY PAVLOVA

Serves: 6

Prep: 35 mins,
plus cooling & chilling

Cook: 1 hour

Ingredients

Meringue
4 egg whites
225 g/8 oz caster sugar
1 tsp cornflour
1 tsp white wine vinegar
1 tsp vanilla extract

Topping
300 ml/10 fl oz double cream
1 tbsp caster sugar
2 tbsp framboise liqueur
175 g/6 oz fresh raspberries
55 g/2 oz plain chocolate shavings

Method

1 Preheat the oven to 150°C/300°F/Gas Mark 2. In a large mixing bowl, whisk the egg whites until stiff and gradually whisk in 115 g/4 oz of the sugar. In a separate bowl, mix the remaining sugar with the cornflour and then whisk it into the egg white mixture; it should be very shiny and firm. Quickly fold the vinegar and vanilla extract into the egg white mixture.

2 Draw a 25-cm/10-inch circle on a sheet of baking paper, turn the paper over and place it on a baking sheet. Pile the meringue onto the baking paper and spread evenly to the edge of the circle; swirl it around on top to make an attractive shape. Bake in the centre of the preheated oven for 1 hour.

3 Remove from the oven, leave to cool slightly, then peel off the paper. Place the meringue on a large serving plate. It will shrink and crack but do not worry about this.

4 An hour before serving, whip together the cream, sugar and liqueur until thick and floppy. Pile on top of the meringue and decorate with the raspberries and chocolate shavings. Chill before serving.

DESSERTS

BAKED ALASKAS

Serves: 4

Prep: 25 mins,
plus freezing

Cook: 5 mins

Ingredients

4 tbsp sultanas or raisins

3 tbsp dark rum or
ginger wine

4 square slices ginger cake

4 scoops vanilla ice cream
or rum and raisin ice cream

3 egg whites

175 g/6 oz caster sugar

Method

1 Preheat the oven to 230°C/450°F/Gas Mark 8.
Mix the sultanas with the rum in a small bowl.

2 Place the cake slices, spaced well apart, on a
baking sheet and scatter a tablespoon of the
soaked sultanas on each slice.

3 Place a scoop of ice cream in the centre of
each slice and place in the freezer.

4 Meanwhile, whisk the egg whites in a clean,
grease-free bowl until soft peaks form.
Gradually whisk the sugar into the egg whites,
a tablespoon at a time, until the mixture forms
stiff peaks.

5 Remove the ice cream-topped cake slices
from the freezer and spoon the meringue over
the ice cream. Spread to cover the ice cream
completely.

6 Bake in the preheated oven for about 5 minutes,
or until starting to brown. Serve immediately.

BROWNIE SUNDAE

Serves: 6

Prep: 30 mins,
plus cooling

Cook: 45–50 mins

Ingredients

175 g/6 oz plain chocolate,
broken into pieces

175 g/6 oz butter,
plus extra for greasing

175 g/6 oz soft light
brown sugar

3 eggs, beaten

115 g/4 oz self-raising flour

Chocolate fudge sauce

55 g/2 oz plain chocolate,
broken into pieces

55 g/2 oz soft light
brown sugar

55 g/2 oz unsalted butter

3 tbsp milk

To serve

6 large scoops of vanilla
ice cream

1 tbsp pecan nuts,
chopped

6 fresh or maraschino
cherries

Method

1 Preheat the oven to 180°C/350°F/Gas Mark 4.
Grease a 20-cm/8-inch square cake tin and line
with baking paper.

2 For the brownie, place the chocolate and butter
in a large heatproof bowl set over a saucepan
of simmering water and heat until melted. Cool
for 5 minutes then whisk in the sugar and eggs.
Sift over the flour and fold in. Pour the mixture
into the prepared cake tin and bake in the
preheated oven for 35–40 minutes, or until risen
and just firm to the touch. Leave to cool in the tin
for 15 minutes, then turn out onto a wire rack to
cool completely.

3 For the sauce, place all the ingredients in a
saucepan and heat gently, stirring all the
time until melted. Bring to the boil and bubble for
1 minute. Remove from the heat and leave
to cool for five minutes.

4 To serve, cut the brownie into six pieces. Place
each piece on a serving plate and top with a
large scoop of ice cream. Spoon over the warm
sauce and decorate with chopped pecan nuts
and cherries.

TOFFEE CHOCOLATE PUFFS

Makes: 12

Prep: 30 mins,
plus chilling & cooling

Cook: 25–30 mins

Ingredients

375 g/13 oz ready-rolled
puff pastry

140 g/5 oz plain chocolate,
broken into pieces

300 ml/10 fl oz double
cream

50 g/1¾ oz caster sugar

4 egg yolks

4 tbsp ready-made
toffee sauce

whipped cream, to serve

cocoa powder, for dusting

Method

1 Line the bases of a 12-cup muffin tin with discs of baking paper. Cut out twelve 5-cm/2-inch rounds from the edge of the pastry and cut the remainder into 12 strips. Roll the strips to half their thickness and line the sides of each hole with 1 strip. Place a disc of pastry in each base and press together to seal and make a tart case. Prick the bases and chill in the refrigerator for 30 minutes.

2 Preheat the oven to 200°C/400°F/Gas Mark 6. While the pastry is chilling, place the chocolate in a heatproof bowl, set the bowl over a saucepan of gently simmering water and heat until melted. Leave to cool slightly, then stir in the cream.

3 Place the sugar and egg yolks in a bowl and beat together, then mix well with the melted chocolate. Place a teaspoon of the toffee sauce into each tart case, then divide the chocolate mixture evenly between the tarts. Bake in the preheated oven for 20–25 minutes, turning the tin around halfway through cooking, until just set. Leave to cool in the tin, then remove carefully and serve with whipped cream, dusted with cocoa.

DESSERTS

HOT ORANGE SOUFFLÉS WITH CHOCOLATE & ORANGE SAUCE

Makes: 12

Prep: 40 mins,
plus cooling

Cook: 25–30 mins

Ingredients

25 g/1 oz unsalted butter,
for greasing

115 g/4 oz caster sugar, plus
2 tbsp for sprinkling

3 eggs, separated,
plus 1 extra egg white

40 g/1½ oz plain flour

225 ml/8 fl oz milk

finely grated rind of
1 large orange

5 tbsp orange juice,
or 3 tbsp orange juice plus
2 tbsp Cointreau

a large pinch of ground
cinnamon

icing sugar, sifted,
for dusting

Sauce

150 g/5½ oz plain
chocolate, roughly
chopped

4 tbsp orange juice

2 tbsp caster sugar

Method

1 Grease twelve x 125-ml/4-fl oz wide-topped ovenproof demitasse coffee cups with the butter, then sprinkle them with 2 tablespoons of caster sugar, tilting to coat them evenly. Put them on a baking tray and set aside.

2 Put half the measured sugar and all the egg yolks into a mixing bowl and beat together for 2 minutes using an electric handheld whisk, until thick and pale. Sift the flour over the surface, then fold it in.

3 Pour the milk into a medium heavy-based saucepan, bring just to the boil, then gradually whisk it into the egg mixture until smooth. Pour the mixture back into the pan, then cook over a low heat, whisking gently, until thickened and smooth.

4 Remove the soufflé mixture from the heat and whisk in the orange rind, orange juice and cinnamon. Cover with clingfilm and leave to cool.

5 Preheat the oven to 190°C/375°F/Gas Mark 5. Whisk the egg whites in a large, clean mixing bowl until you have stiff, moist-looking peaks. Gradually whisk in the remaining sugar, a teaspoon at a time. Fold the whites into the cooled soufflé mixture, then divide between the

DESSERTS

12 cups so that they are three-quarters full. Bake in the preheated oven for 15–20 minutes, or until the soufflés are well risen, the tops are golden and they are almost set in the centre.

6 Meanwhile, to make the sauce, put the chocolate, orange juice and sugar in a heatproof bowl, set the bowl over a saucepan of gently simmering water and heat until smooth and melted, stirring from time to time. Pour into a jug.

7 Quickly serve the soufflés on saucers, dust with sifted icing sugar and drizzle the warm chocolate sauce over the top.

CAPPUCCINO SOUFFLÉS

Makes: 6   **Prep: 30 mins**   **Cook: 25 mins**

Ingredients

6 tbsp whipping cream

2 tsp instant espresso coffee granules

2 tbsp coffee liqueur

butter, for greasing

3 large eggs, separated, plus 1 extra egg white

2 tbsp golden caster sugar, plus extra for coating

150 g/5½ oz plain chocolate, melted and cooled

cocoa powder, for dusting

Method

1 Place the cream in a small, heavy-based saucepan and heat gently. Stir in the coffee until it has dissolved, then stir in the coffee liqueur. Divide the coffee mixture between six lightly greased 175-ml/6-fl oz ramekins coated with caster sugar. Preheat the oven to 190°C/375°F/ Gas Mark 5.

2 Place the egg whites in a clean, grease-free bowl and whisk until soft peaks form, then gradually whisk in the sugar until stiff but not dry. Stir the egg yolks and melted chocolate together in a separate bowl, then stir in a little of the whisked egg whites. Gradually fold in the remaining egg whites.

3 Divide the mixture between the prepared ramekins. Place the ramekins on a baking sheet and bake in the preheated oven for 15 minutes, or until just set. Dust with sifted cocoa powder and serve immediately.

DESSERTS

LEMON & CHOCOLATE TART

Serves: 8

Prep: 30 mins, plus chilling & cooling

Cook: 1¼ hours

Ingredients

115 g/4 oz plain flour

25 g/1 oz cocoa powder

75 g/2¾ oz butter

25 g/1 oz ground almonds

150 g/1¾ oz golden caster sugar

1 egg, beaten

chocolate caraque, to decorate

Filling

4 eggs

1 egg yolk

200 g/7 oz golden caster sugar

150 ml/5 fl oz double cream

grated rind and juice of 2 lemons

Method

1 Sift the flour and cocoa into a food processor. Add the butter, ground almonds, sugar and egg and process until the mixture forms a dough. Gather the dough together and press into a flattened ball. Place in the centre of a 20-cm/ 8-inch loose-based tart tin and press evenly over the base of the tin with your fingers, then work the pastry up the sides with your thumbs. Allow any excess pastry to go over the edge. Cover and leave to chill for 30 minutes.

2 Preheat the oven to 200°C/400°F/Gas Mark 6. Trim off the excess pastry. Prick the base lightly with a fork, then line with baking paper and fill with baking beans. Bake in the oven for 12–15 minutes, or until the pastry no longer looks raw. Remove the beans and paper, then return the pastry case to the oven and bake for a further 10 minutes, or until the pastry is firm. Remove to cool. Reduce the oven temperature to 150°C/300°F/Gas Mark 2.

3 To make the filling, whisk the whole eggs, egg yolk and sugar together until smooth. Add the cream and whisk again, then stir in the lemon rind and juice. Pour the filling into the pastry case and bake for 50 minutes, or until just set. When the tart is cooked, remove from the tin and leave to cool. Decorate with chocolate caraque to serve.

DESSERTS

SUMMER FRUIT TARTLETS

Makes: 12 **Prep: 30 mins,** plus chilling **Cook: 15–20 mins**

Ingredients

200 g/7 oz plain flour, plus extra for dusting

85 g/3 oz icing sugar, sifted

55 g/2 oz ground almonds

115 g/4 oz butter

1 egg yolk

1 tbsp milk

350 g/12 oz fresh summer berries, including strawberries

Filling

225 g/8 oz cream cheese

icing sugar, to taste, plus extra, sifted, for dusting

Method

1 Sift the flour and icing sugar into a bowl. Stir in the ground almonds. Add the butter, rubbing in until the mixture resembles breadcrumbs. Add the egg yolk and milk and work in until the dough binds together. Wrap in clingfilm and chill for 30 minutes.

2 Preheat the oven to 200°C/400°F/Gas Mark 6. Roll out the dough on a lightly floured surface and use it to line 12 deep tartlet tins. Prick the bases and press a piece of foil into each.

3 Bake in the preheated oven for 10–15 minutes, or until light golden brown. Remove the foil and bake for a further 2–3 minutes. Transfer to a wire rack to cool.

4 Halve the strawberries. For the filling, place the cream cheese and icing sugar in a bowl and mix together. Place a spoonful of filling in each tartlet and arrange the berries on top.

5 Dust with sifted icing sugar and serve immediately.

CHOCOLATE FONDANT PUDDINGS

Makes: 4

Prep: 25 mins, plus cooling

Cook: 15–20 mins, plus standing

Ingredients

100 g/3½ oz butter, plus extra for greasing

100 g/3½ oz plain chocolate, broken into pieces

2 large eggs

1 tsp vanilla extract

100 g/3½ oz golden caster sugar, plus extra for sprinkling

2 tbsp plain flour

icing sugar, for dusting

lightly whipped cream, to serve

Method

1 Preheat the oven to 200°C/400°F/Gas Mark 6. Grease four x 175-ml/6-fl oz ramekin dishes and sprinkle with caster sugar.

2 Place the butter and chocolate in a heatproof bowl set over a saucepan of gently simmering water until melted. Stir until smooth. Leave to cool.

3 Place the eggs, vanilla extract, caster sugar and flour in a bowl and whisk together. Stir in the melted chocolate mixture. Pour into the prepared ramekins and place on a baking sheet. Bake in the preheated oven for 12–15 minutes, or until the puddings are well risen and set on the outside but still molten inside.

4 Leave to stand for 1 minute, then turn the puddings out onto serving plates. Dust with icing sugar and serve immediately with whipped cream.

DESSERTS

BLACK FOREST GATEAU

Serves: 12

Prep: 50 mins,
plus cooling & chilling

Cook: 25–30 mins

Ingredients

6 eggs, separated

6 tbsp warm water

pinch of salt

200 g/7 oz caster sugar

2 tsp vanilla extract

300 g/10½ oz self-raising flour

1 tbsp cocoa powder

6 tbsp kirsch

55 g/2 oz grated dark chocolate, for decorating

Filling

350 g/12 oz morello cherries from a jar

1½ tbsp caster sugar

1 tbsp cornflour

600 ml/1 pint whipping cream

2 tsp vanilla extract

Method

1 Preheat the oven to 200°C/400°F/Gas Mark 6. Line a 28-cm/11-inch round springform cake tin with baking paper.

2 To make the cake, put the egg whites, water and salt in a bowl and, using an electric mixer, whisk until light and fluffy. Gradually whisk in the caster sugar and continue beating. Mix in the egg yolks and vanilla extract. Sift together the flour and cocoa powder into another bowl, then add to the egg mixture and fold in gently.

3 Pour the mixture into the cake tin and bake in the preheated oven for about 20–25 minutes until risen and just firm to the touch. Turn out onto a wire rack to cool, and remove the baking paper.

4 Cut the sponge horizontally into three equal layers. Drizzle 2 tablespoons of the kirsch over each layer.

5 To make the filling, drain the morello cherries in a sieve, reserving the juice. Bring the cherry juice to the boil in a small saucepan with ½ tablespoon of the caster sugar. Combine the cornflour with a little water, stir into the cherry juice until dissolved and thickened. Add the cherries, remove from the hob, and leave to cool. Whip the cream with the vanilla extract and the remaining caster sugar until firmly peaking.

DESSERTS

6 Spread a third of the whipped cream on the bottom cake layer, then arrange half of the cherries on top. Position the second layer on top, and spread with cream and cherries as above. Finally place the third layer on top. Spread whipped cream over the whole cake. Use a palette knife to coat the sides of the gateau with grated chocolate and scatter the rest over the top. Chill in the refrigerator for at least one hour before serving.

ALMOND & HAZELNUT GATEAU

Serves: 8

Prep: 40 mins, plus cooling, setting & chilling

Cook: 20–25 mins

Ingredients

butter, for greasing

4 eggs

115 g/4 oz caster sugar

50 g/1¾ oz ground almonds

50 g/1¾ oz ground hazelnuts

50 g/1¾ oz plain flour

70 g/2½ oz flaked almonds

icing sugar, for dusting

Filling

100 g/3½ oz plain chocolate, broken into pieces

1 tbsp butter

300 ml/10 fl oz double cream

Method

1 Preheat the oven to 190°C/375°F/Gas Mark 5. Grease two 18-cm/7-inch sandwich tins and line with baking paper. Whisk the eggs and caster sugar in a large mixing bowl with an electric hand-held whisk for about 10 minutes, or until the mixture is very light and foamy and a trail is left when the whisk is dragged across the surface. Fold in the ground nuts. Sift the flour and fold in with a metal spoon or palette knife. Divide the mixture between the prepared tins.

2 Scatter the flaked almonds over the top of one of the cakes. Bake both of the cakes in the oven for 15–20 minutes, or until springy to the touch. Leave to cool slightly in the tins. Remove the cakes from the tins and transfer to a wire rack to cool.

3 To make the filling, melt the chocolate in a heatproof bowl set over a saucepan of gently simmering water, remove from the heat and stir in the butter. Leave the mixture to cool slightly. Whip the cream until just holding its shape, then fold in the melted chocolate mixture. Place the cake without the flaked almonds on a serving plate and spread the filling over it. Leave the filling to set slightly, then place the almond-topped cake on top and chill for about 1 hour. Dust with icing sugar and serve.

DESSERTS

MINI CHOCOLATE ÉCLAIRS WITH IRISH CREAM

Makes: 36 (approximately)

Prep: 45 mins, plus cooling & setting

Cook: 25–30 mins

Ingredients

55 g/2 oz unsalted butter, plus extra for greasing

150 ml/5 fl oz water

70 g/2½ oz plain flour

pinch of salt

2 eggs, beaten

a few drops of vanilla extract

Filling

350 ml/12 fl oz double cream

2 tbsp icing sugar, sifted

4 tbsp Irish cream liqueur

Topping

25 g/1 oz unsalted butter, diced

100 g/3½ oz plain chocolate, roughly chopped

1 tbsp icing sugar, sifted

2 tsp milk

Method

1 Preheat the oven to 200°C/400°F/Gas Mark 6. Lightly grease two baking trays.

2 Put the butter and water into a medium heavy-based saucepan and heat gently until the butter has melted. Increase the heat and bring to the boil, then remove from the heat. Sift in the flour and salt, then return the pan to the heat and stir together until the mixture makes a smooth ball that leaves the sides of the pan clean. Leave to cool for at least 15 minutes.

3 Gradually beat in the eggs, beating well after each addition, until the mixture is smooth. Stir in the vanilla extract. Spoon the mixture into a large piping bag fitted with a 1.5-cm/⅝-inch plain piping nozzle, then pipe 4-cm/1½-inch long éclairs onto the prepared baking trays.

4 Bake in the preheated oven for 10–12 minutes, until well risen and crisp on the outside. Make a slit in the side of each éclair to allow the steam to escape, then put them back in the oven for 2 minutes. Leave to cool.

5 About an hour before serving, make the filling. Pour the cream into a large mixing bowl, add the sifted icing sugar and cream liqueur, and

whisk until it forms soft swirls. Spoon this into a piping bag fitted with a star tube, then pipe it into the éclairs.

6 For the topping, put all the ingredients in a heatproof bowl, set the bowl over a heavy-based saucepan of gently simmering water and heat until melted, smooth and glossy, stirring once or twice. Spoon this over the éclairs, leave to set for 15 minutes, then transfer to a serving plate.

LEMON TART

Serves: 6-8

Prep: 35 mins, plus chilling & cooling

Cook: 1¼ hours

Ingredients

Pastry

200 g/7 oz plain flour, plus extra for dusting

90 g/3¼ oz icing sugar

90 g/3¼ oz ground almonds

140 g/5 oz butter, plus extra for greasing

1 egg

pinch of salt

Filling

grated rind and juice of 3 lemons

150 g/5½ oz butter

265 g/9½ oz caster sugar

4 eggs

Topping

2 lemons, thinly sliced

100 ml/3½ fl oz water

100 g/3½ oz caster sugar

Method

1 To make the pastry, mix together the flour, icing sugar and ground almonds. Melt the butter in a saucepan. Combine the flour mixture with the butter, egg and salt in a food processer, then knead by hand until a smooth dough forms. Wrap in clingfilm and chill in the refrigerator for 30 minutes.

2 Preheat the oven to 180°C/350°F/Gas Mark 4. Grease a 24-cm/9½-inch round tart tin.

3 To make the filling, put the lemon rind and juice, butter and sugar into a saucepan over a low heat and heat, stirring constantly, until the sugar has dissolved. Whisk the eggs with a balloon whisk until frothy, then add them to the lemon mixture. Remove from the heat and continue stirring until smooth and creamy.

4 Roll out the dough on a work surface lightly dusted with flour into a 5-mm/¼-inch thick round. Lay it in the tart tin, pressing it into place and trimming off any surplus with a sharp knife. Prick the base with a fork in several places.

5 Line with baking paper, fill with baking beans and bake on the bottom shelf of the preheated oven for 15 minutes. Remove the beans and paper and bake for a further 15 minutes. Remove from the oven and reduce the oven

temperature to 140°C/275°F/Gas Mark 1. Pour the filling into the pastry case and bake for a further 35 minutes. Transfer to a wire rack to cool.

6   Meanwhile, to make the topping, put the lemon slices into a shallow saucepan, add the water and sugar, bring to the boil and simmer for 10 minutes. Remove from the heat and leave to cool.

7   Arrange the lemon slices on top of the tart and serve.

TARTE TATIN

Serves: 6

Prep: 30 mins,
plus resting

Cook: 35–50 mins

Ingredients

200 g/7 oz caster sugar

150 g/5½ oz unsalted butter

800 g/1 lb 12 oz Cox or
Golden Delicious apples

350 g/12 oz ready-made
puff pastry

Method

1 Place a 20-cm/8-inch ovenproof frying pan over
a low heat and add the sugar. Melt the sugar until
it starts to caramelize. Do not let it burn. Add the
butter and stir it in to make a light toffee sauce.
Remove from the heat.

2 Peel the apples and cut them into eighths
vertically. Core the apples and lay them in the
pan on top of the toffee sauce, on their sides.
They should fill the pan. If there are any large gaps
add a few more apple pieces. Put the pan over
a medium heat and cover. Simmer, without
stirring, for about 5–10 minutes until the apples
have soaked up some of the sauce. Remove
from the heat.

3 Preheat the oven to 190°C/375°F/Gas Mark 5.
Roll out the pastry so that it will thickly cover the
pan, with extra overhanging the sides. Lay it on
top of the apples and tuck the edges down inside
between the fruit and the pan until it is sealed.
Don't worry about making it look too neat – it will
be turned over before serving. Put the pan into
the oven and bake for 25–35 minutes, checking to
ensure the pastry doesn't burn. The pastry should
be puffed and golden. Remove from the oven
and leave for 30–60 minutes. To serve, ensure
the tart is a little warm. Place a plate on top of the
frying pan. Carefully turn it over and lift the pan off.
Serve warm.

DESSERTS

APPLE & CIDER TART

Serves: 6–8

Prep: 45 mins,
plus cooling

Cook: 50 mins

Ingredients

Pastry

300 g/10½ oz plain flour,
plus extra for dusting

1 tsp baking powder

100 g/3½ oz butter,
plus extra for greasing

150 g/5½ oz low-fat curd
cheese

100 ml/3½ fl oz milk

80 g/2¾ oz caster sugar

1 tsp vanilla sugar

pinch of salt

Filling

1 sachet vanilla
blancmange powder

2 eggs, separated

350 ml/12 fl oz milk

100 g/3½ oz caster sugar

150 ml/5 fl oz cider

pinch of salt

750 g/1 lb 10 oz Golden
Delicious apples

juice of ½ lemon

whipped cream, to serve
(optional)

Method

1 Preheat the oven to 180°C/350°F/Gas Mark 4.
Grease a 26-cm/10½-inch round tart tin.

2 To make the pastry, sift together the flour and the
baking powder. Melt the butter in a saucepan.
Put the flour mixture into the bowl of a food
mixer with the curd cheese, milk, butter, caster
sugar, vanilla sugar and salt and mix to a smooth
dough. Roll out the pastry on a work surface
lightly dusted with flour to a round slightly larger
than the tin. Line the prepared tin with the pastry
turning up the edge.

3 To make the filling, mix the blancmange powder
with the egg yolks and 4 tablespoons of the milk.
Pour the remaining milk into a saucepan with
80 g/2¾ oz of the sugar and bring to the boil.
Pour in the blancmange powder mixture, stirring,
and bring back to the boil. Add the cider and
bring back to the boil. Transfer the mixture to a
bowl, cover with clingfilm and leave to cool in
the refrigerator until lukewarm.

4 Meanwhile, whisk the egg whites with the salt
until they hold stiff peaks, then fold into the
lukewarm blancmange mixture. Spread the
mixture over the pastry and level the surface.

5 Peel, core and quarter the apples and cut
them into thin slices. Mix the apple slices with

the remaining sugar and the lemon juice, then arrange on top of the blancmange mixture in a circular pattern.

6 Bake in the preheated oven for about 35 minutes until golden yellow. Leave to cool before serving with whipped cream, if using.

SALTED CARAMEL MINI ÉCLAIRS

Makes: 30 (approximately)

Prep: 55 mins, plus cooling & setting

Cook: 35 mins

Ingredients

50 g/1¾ oz butter

150 ml/5 fl oz water

70 g/2½ oz plain flour, sifted

pinch of salt

2 eggs, beaten

Caramel glaze

150 g/5½ oz granulated sugar

3 tbsp cold water

70 g/2½ oz lightly salted butter

pinch of sea salt

4 tbsp double cream

To assemble

300 ml/10 fl oz double cream

2 tsp coffee and chicory extract

1 sheet edible gold leaf or 1 tbsp gold hundreds and thousands

Method

1 Preheat the oven to 220°C/425°F/Gas Mark 7. Line two large baking sheets with baking paper.

2 To make the pastry, put the butter and water into a saucepan and heat gently until the butter has melted. Bring to a rolling boil, remove from the heat and quickly beat in the flour and salt until the mixture forms a ball that leaves the sides of the pan clean. Transfer to a bowl and leave to cool for 5 minutes.

3 Gradually beat in the eggs to form a smooth, glossy mixture with a soft dropping consistency. Spoon into a piping bag fitted with a 1-cm/ ½-inch plain nozzle and pipe fifteen 7-cm/ 2¾-inch mini éclairs onto each of the prepared baking sheets. Sprinkle a little water around the éclairs.

4 Bake in the preheated oven for 15 minutes, or until golden. Remove from the oven and use the tip of a knife to pierce a hole in the end of each éclair. Return to the oven for a further 5 minutes. Transfer to a wire rack and leave to cool completely.

5 To make the glaze, put the sugar and water into a heavy-based saucepan. Heat gently, stirring, until the sugar has dissolved, then bring to the boil and continue boiling, without stirring, until a deep golden caramel forms. Remove from the

heat and leave to stand for 2 minutes, then stir in the butter and salt. Use a balloon whisk to whisk in the double cream and continue whisking until you have a smooth caramel sauce. Pour into a heatproof bowl and leave to cool and thicken for about 30 minutes, stirring occasionally.

6 To assemble the éclairs, put the cream into a bowl with the coffee and chicory extract and whip until it holds soft peaks. Spoon into a piping bag fitted with a 5-mm/¼-inch plain nozzle. Use the tip of a knife to make the holes at the end of each éclair a little larger. Pipe the cream into the éclairs through the holes.

7 Gently dip the top of each filled éclair in the caramel and place on a wire rack. Use the tip of a fine paintbrush to dot a few tiny specks of gold leaf onto the caramel. Leave in a cool place to set before serving.

BANANA & CHOCOLATE FLAN

Serves: 6–8

Prep: 45 mins,
plus chilling & soaking

Cook: 10 mins

Ingredients

Base

150 g/5½ oz plain chocolate

20 g/¾ oz butter

150 g/5½ oz chocolate puffed rice cereal

Topping

600 g/1 lb 5 oz low-fat curd cheese

100 g/3½ oz caster sugar

1 tsp vanilla sugar

grated rind of 1 lemon

3 ripe bananas, around 350 g/12 oz (peeled weight)

2 tbsp lemon juice

10 sheets leaf gelatine

200 ml/7 fl oz whipping cream

250 g/9 oz plain chocolate shavings

Method

1. Line a 28-cm/11-inch round springform tin with baking paper. To make the base, break the chocolate into pieces, put it into a heatproof bowl set over a saucepan of gently simmering water, add the butter and heat until melted, stirring constantly. Whizz the cereal in a food processor and stir into the chocolate mixture. Spoon the chocolate mixture into the prepared tin, pressing down well with the back of the spoon. Leave to chill in the refrigerator for 1 hour.

2. To make the topping, mix together the curd cheese, caster sugar, vanilla sugar and lemon rind in a bowl. Thinly slice the bananas and drizzle with the lemon juice. Soak the gelatine in cold water for 10 minutes, then gently squeeze out the water. Put the gelatine into a saucepan with a little water and stir over a medium heat until dissolved. Add the bananas and gelatine to the curd cheese mixture.

3. Whip the cream until it holds soft peaks, then use a spatula to fold it into the setting curd cheese and banana mixture. Spread the mixture over the base and level the surface with a palette knife. Leave to chill in the refrigerator for 2 hours. Sprinkle the chocolate shavings over the flan. Unclip and release the springform, transfer to a cake plate and serve.

DESSERTS

CHOCOLATE NUT STRUDEL

Serves: 6   **Prep: 30 mins**   **Cook: 20–25 mins**

Ingredients

200 g/7 oz mixed chopped nuts

115 g/4 oz plain chocolate, chopped

115 g/4 oz milk chocolate, chopped

115 g/4 oz white chocolate, chopped

200 g/7 oz filo pastry, thawed if frozen

150 g/5½ oz butter, melted, plus extra for greasing

3 tbsp golden syrup

Method

1 Preheat the oven to 190°C/375°F/Gas Mark 5. Grease a baking sheet.

2 Reserve 1 tablespoon of the nuts. Place the remaining nuts in a bowl and mix together with the three types of chocolate.

3 Place a sheet of filo pastry on a clean tea towel. Brush the sheet of filo pastry with the melted butter, drizzle with a little golden syrup and sprinkle with a little of the nut and chocolate mixture. Repeat the layers until you have used up all the filo pastry, butter, nuts and chocolate and most of the golden syrup.

4 Use the tea towel to help you carefully roll up the strudel and place on the prepared baking sheet. Drizzle with a little more golden syrup and sprinkle with the reserved nuts. Bake in the preheated oven for 20–25 minutes. If the nuts start to brown too much, cover the strudel with a sheet of foil. Serve warm.

DESSERTS

PLUM STRUDEL

Serves: 6–8

Prep: 35 mins, plus resting

Cook: 50 mins

Ingredients

Pastry

130 ml/4¼ fl oz cold water

pinch of salt

1 tbsp sunflower oil, plus extra for brushing

1 egg yolk

250 g/9 oz plain flour, plus extra for dusting

melted butter, for greasing

fruit brandy such as plum brandy or Calvados, for drizzling

icing sugar, for dusting

Filling

400 g/14 oz plums

180 g/6¼ oz butter

100 g/3½ oz dried breadcrumbs

70 g/2½ oz ground almonds

150 g/5½ oz caster sugar

pinch of ground cinnamon

Method

1 To make the pastry, mix together the water, salt, oil and egg yolk in a mixing bowl. Add the flour and mix until smooth. Cover the dough and leave to rest for 30 minutes.

2 Turn out the pastry onto a tea towel lightly dusted with flour. Roll the pastry out as thinly as possible then, using the back of your hands, gently stretch it out. Brush with oil and a little melted butter, then drizzle with the brandy.

3 Preheat the oven to 180°C/350°F/Gas Mark 4. Grease a 30 x 40-cm/12 x 16-inch baking tray.

4 To make the filling, stone the plums, cut them into small slices and arrange on top of the pastry, leaving a small border. Melt half the butter in a frying pan, add the breadcrumbs and sauté until brown. Mix with the ground almonds, caster sugar and cinnamon and scatter the mixture over the plums.

5 Use the tea towel to roll up the pastry and lay it in the prepared baking tray, gently curving it around the edges. Bake in the preheated oven for about 45 minutes. Meanwhile, melt the remaining butter and use to brush the strudel shortly before the end of cooking. Serve warm, dusted with icing sugar.

BABY BLUEBERRY BRÛLÉES

Makes: 12

Prep: 20 mins,
plus cooling & chilling

Cook: 25 mins

Ingredients

125 g/4½ oz blueberries

4 egg yolks

1 tsp vanilla extract

100 g/3½ oz caster sugar

300 ml/10 fl oz double cream

Method

1 Preheat the oven to 160°C/325°F/Gas Mark 3. Put twelve x 60-ml/2-fl oz ovenproof dishes in a large roasting tin and divide the blueberries between them.

2 Put the egg yolks, vanilla extract and 40 g/1½ oz of the sugar into a jug and mix together using a fork until smooth and creamy. Pour the cream into a small heavy-based saucepan, bring to the boil, then gradually mix it into the yolks. Strain the mixture through a sieve back into the pan before pouring it back into the jug.

3 Pour the cream mixture over the blueberries. Pour warm water into the roasting tin to come halfway up the sides of the dishes. Bake in the preheated oven for 15 minutes, or until the custard is just set, with a slight wobble in the centre.

4 Allow to cool for 5–10 minutes, then lift the dishes out of the water and transfer to the refrigerator to chill for 3–4 hours.

5 To serve, sprinkle the remaining sugar over the dishes in an even layer, then caramelize it using a cook's blow torch or under a grill preheated to hot.

DESSERTS

BREAD PUDDING

Serves: 8

Prep: 30 mins,
plus chilling & standing

Cook: 1 hour 40 mins

Ingredients

600 ml/1 pint milk

115 g/4 oz butter, diced,
plus extra for greasing

1 tbsp mixed spice

¼ tsp ground cloves

½ tsp ground nutmeg

18 slices day-old white
bread, torn into pieces

350 g/12 oz soft light
brown sugar, plus 2 tbsp
extra for sprinkling

425 g/15 oz mixed dried
fruit, such as sultanas,
raisins and currants

4 tbsp finely chopped
ready-to-eat dried apricots

2 extra large eggs, beaten

finely grated zest of
½ lemon

Rum sauce

140 g/5 oz icing sugar

70 g/2½ oz soft light
brown sugar

150 g/5½ oz butter,
softened

4 tsp milk

2 tbsp light or dark rum

finely grated zest of
½ lemon

Method

1 To make the sauce, sift the icing sugar and brown sugar into a small bowl and set aside. Beat the butter in another bowl until it is soft and creamy. Gradually beat the sugars into the butter, alternating with the milk and rum. Stir in the lemon zest, taking care not to overbeat or the mixture will separate. Transfer the sauce to a serving bowl, cover and chill for at least 30 minutes until firm.

2 Put the milk, butter and spices into a large saucepan over a medium heat and heat until small bubbles appear. Add the bread, brown sugar, mixed dried fruit and apricots and stir together until well blended and the bread starts to break down. Remove from the heat and leave to stand for 20 minutes.

3 Meanwhile, preheat the oven to 180°C/350°F/ Gas Mark 4 and grease a 20-cm/8-inch square baking dish. Stir the pudding mixture again to distribute the fruit evenly. Stir in the eggs and lemon zest. Spoon the mixture into the prepared dish, smooth the surface and sprinkle with brown sugar.

4 Bake in the preheated oven for 1½ hours, or until it is set and crusty on top. Cut into pieces and serve immediately with the sauce.

DESSERTS

BAKED APPLES

Makes: 4   **Prep: 20 mins**   **Cook: 45–50 mins**

Ingredients

4 cooking apples
1 tbsp lemon juice
50 g/1¾ oz blueberries
50 g/1¾ oz raisins
25 g/1 oz mixed nuts, chopped and toasted
½ tsp ground cinnamon
2 tbsp soft brown sugar
275 ml/9½ fl oz red wine
2 tsp cornflour
4 tsp water
double cream, to serve (optional)

Method

1 Preheat the oven to 200°C/400°F/Gas Mark 6. Using a sharp knife, score a line around the centre of each apple. Core the apples, then brush the centres with the lemon juice to prevent discoloration. Transfer them to a small roasting tin.

2 Place the blueberries and raisins in a bowl, then add the nuts, cinnamon and sugar. Mix together well. Pile the mixture into the centres of the apples, then pour over the wine.

3 Transfer the stuffed apples to the preheated oven and bake for 40–45 minutes, or until tender. Remove from the oven, then lift the apples out of the roasting tin and keep them warm.

4 Blend the cornflour with the water, then add the mixture to the cooking juices in the roasting tin. Transfer to the hob and cook over a medium heat, stirring, until thickened. Remove from the heat and pour over the apples. Serve the apples with double cream, if using.

★ **Variation**

Bake the apples in elderflower wine or grape juice instead of red wine.

BREADS & SWEET PIES

FIVE-GRAIN LOAF

Makes: 1 loaf

Prep: 25 mins,
plus rising & cooling

Cook: 25–30 mins

Ingredients

300 g/10½ oz strong
wholemeal flour,
plus extra for dusting

225 g/8 oz strong white flour

1 tsp salt

100 g/3½ oz five-seed mix
(including sesame,
pumpkin, sunflower,
hemp and linseeds)

7 g/¼ oz easy-blend
dried yeast

1 tbsp soft light brown sugar

2 tbsp sunflower oil,
plus extra for greasing

300 ml/10 fl oz lukewarm
water

Method

1 Lightly grease a baking sheet with oil. Mix the
wholemeal flour, white flour, salt, seed mix
and yeast in a large bowl. Stir in the sugar. Mix
together the oil and water. Make a well in the
centre and pour in the liquid. Mix with a knife to
make a soft sticky dough.

2 Turn out the dough onto a lightly floured work
surface and knead for 5–7 minutes, or until
smooth and elastic. Shape the dough into a
round ball and place on the prepared baking
sheet. Dust the top of the loaf with wholemeal
flour and leave in a warm place for 1–1½ hours,
or until doubled in size.

3 Meanwhile, preheat the oven to 220°C/425°F/
Gas Mark 7. Bake in the preheated oven for
5 minutes. Reduce the oven temperature to
200°C/400°F/Gas Mark 6 and bake for a further
20–25 minutes, or until golden brown and the
base sounds hollow when tapped with your
knuckles. Transfer to a wire rack to cool.

★ Variation

To make individual rolls, divide and shape the
dough into 12 round balls and bake for
10–15 minutes at 200°C/400°F/Gas Mark 6.

WHOLEMEAL LOAF

Makes: 1 loaf

Prep: 30 mins,
plus rising & cooling

Cook: 30 mins

Ingredients

225 g/8 oz strong
wholemeal flour,
plus extra for dusting

1 tbsp skimmed
milk powder

1 tsp salt

2 tbsp soft light brown sugar

1 tsp easy-blend dried yeast

1½ tbsp sunflower oil,
plus extra for greasing

175 ml/6 fl oz lukewarm
water

Method

1. Place the flour, milk powder, salt, sugar and yeast in a large bowl. Pour in the oil and add the water, then mix well to make a smooth dough.

2. Turn out onto a lightly floured surface and knead well for about 10 minutes, or until smooth. Brush a bowl with oil. Shape the dough into a ball, place it in the bowl and cover with a damp tea towel. Leave to rise in a warm place for 1 hour, or until the dough has doubled in volume.

3. Preheat the oven to 220°C/425°F/Gas Mark 7. Oil a 900-g/2-lb loaf tin. Turn the dough out onto a lightly floured surface and knead for 1 minute, or until smooth. Shape the dough the length of the tin and three times the width. Fold the dough into three lengthways and place it in the tin with the join underneath. Cover and leave in a warm place for 30 minutes, or until it has risen above the tin.

4. Place in the preheated oven and bake for 30 minutes, or until firm and golden brown. Test that the loaf is cooked by tapping on the base with your knuckles – it should sound hollow. Transfer to a wire rack to cool.

CRUSTY WHITE LOAF

Makes: 1 loaf

Prep: 35 mins,
plus rising & cooling

Cook: 30 mins

Ingredients

1 egg

1 egg yolk

150–200 ml/5–7 fl oz lukewarm water

500 g/1 lb 2 oz strong white flour, plus extra for dusting

1½ tsp salt

2 tsp white sugar

1 tsp easy-blend dried yeast

25 g/1 oz butter, diced

sunflower oil, for greasing

Method

1 Place the egg and egg yolk in a jug and beat lightly to mix. Add enough lukewarm water to make up to 300 ml/10 fl oz. Stir well.

2 Place the flour, salt, sugar and yeast in a large bowl. Add the butter and rub it in with your fingertips until the mixture resembles breadcrumbs. Make a well in the centre, add the egg mixture and work to a smooth dough.

3 Turn out onto a lightly floured surface and knead well for about 10 minutes, or until smooth. Brush a bowl with oil. Shape the dough into a ball, place it in the bowl and cover with a damp tea towel. Leave to rise in a warm place for 1 hour, or until the dough has doubled in volume. Preheat the oven to 220°C/425°F/Gas Mark 7. Oil a 900-g/2-lb loaf tin. Turn out the dough onto a lightly floured surface and knead for 1 minute, or until smooth. Shape the dough the length of the tin and three times the width. Fold the dough into three lengthways and place it in the tin with the join underneath. Cover and leave in a warm place for 30 minutes, or until it has risen above the tin.

4 Place in the preheated oven and bake for 30 minutes, or until firm and golden brown. Test that the loaf is cooked by tapping on the base with your knuckles – it should sound hollow. Transfer to a wire rack to cool.

BREADS & SWEET PIES

BAGUETTE

Makes: 2 loaves

Prep: 55 mins, plus rising, resting & cooling

Cook: 15–20 mins

Ingredients

450 g/1 lb strong white flour, plus extra for dusting

1½ tsp salt

10 g/¼ oz easy-blend dried yeast

325 ml/11 fl oz lukewarm water

vegetable oil, for brushing

Method

1 Sift the flour and salt together into a bowl and stir in the yeast. Make a well in the centre and pour in the lukewarm water. Stir well with a wooden spoon until the dough begins to come together, then knead with your hands until it leaves the side of the bowl. Turn out on to a lightly floured surface and knead well for about 10 minutes, or until smooth and elastic. Brush a bowl with oil. Shape the dough into a ball, put it in the bowl and put the bowl into a plastic bag or cover with a damp tea towel. Leave to rise in a warm place for 1 hour, or until the dough has doubled in volume.

2 Turn out the dough on to a lightly floured surface, knock back with your fist and knead for 1–2 minutes. Cut the dough in half and shape each piece into a ball. Roll out each ball to a rectangle measuring 7.5 x 20 cm/3 x 8 inches. From one long side of a dough rectangle, fold one-third of the dough down, then fold over the remaining third of the dough. Press gently. Fold the second dough rectangle in the same way. Put both loaves in plastic bags or cover with damp tea towels and leave to rest for 10 minutes. Repeat the rolling and folding twice more, leaving the dough to rest for 10 minutes each time.

3 Lightly flour and pleat two tea towels or flour two bannetons. Gently roll and stretch each piece of dough until it is 30 cm/12 inches long and an even thickness. Support each loaf on the pleated tea towels or in the bannetons, cover with damp tea towels and leave to rise for 30–40 minutes. Preheat the oven to 230°C/450°F/Gas Mark 8. Brush a large baking sheet with oil. Carefully roll the loaves on to the baking sheets and slash the tops several times with a sharp knife. Bake in the preheated oven for 15–20 minutes, or until golden brown. Transfer to a wire rack to cool before serving.

SPICED FRUIT LOAF

Makes: 1 loaf

Prep: 25 mins,
plus rising & cooling

Cook: 1¼ hours

Ingredients

450 g/1 lb strong white flour,
plus extra for dusting

pinch of salt

2 tsp mixed spice

115 g/4 oz unsalted butter,
diced

7 g/¼ oz easy-blend
dried yeast

115 g/4 oz unrefined
caster sugar

115 g/4 oz currants

115 g/4 oz raisins

50 g/1¾ oz mixed peel,
chopped

finely grated rind of
1 orange

1 egg, beaten

150 ml/5 fl oz milk, warmed

vegetable oil, for oiling

Method

1 Sift the flour, salt and mixed spice into a bowl
and rub in the butter until the mixture resembles
breadcrumbs. Stir in the yeast, sugar, dried fruit,
mixed peel and orange rind, then add the egg
and the warm milk and bring together to form a
soft dough.

2 Knead the dough briefly on a lightly floured work
surface. Flour a clean bowl and add the dough.
Cover the bowl and leave to rise in a warm
place for 2 hours.

3 Preheat the oven to 180°C/350°F/Gas Mark 4
and oil a 900-g/2-lb loaf tin. Knead the dough
again briefly, then place it in the prepared tin,
cover and leave to rise for 20 minutes. Bake in
the preheated oven for 1 hour 10 minutes – the
loaf should be golden and well risen. Leave to
cool in the tin before slicing and serving.

SEEDED RYE BREAD

Makes: 1 loaf

Prep: 30 mins,
plus rising & cooling

Cook: 30–35 mins

Ingredients

250 g/9 oz rye flour,
plus extra for dusting

250 g/9 oz strong white flour

1½ tsp salt

1 tbsp caraway seeds

7 g/¼ oz easy-blend
dried yeast

25 g/1 oz butter, melted

2 tbsp honey, warmed

300 ml/10 fl oz lukewarm
water

sunflower oil, for greasing

Method

1 Mix the rye flour, white flour, salt, caraway seeds and yeast in a large bowl and make a well in the centre. Mix together the butter, honey and water and pour into the well. Mix with a knife to make a soft, sticky dough. Lightly grease a baking sheet with oil.

2 Turn out the dough onto a floured work surface and knead for 10 minutes, or until smooth and elastic. Shape into an oval and place on the prepared baking sheet. Slash the top of the loaf in a diamond pattern, lightly dust with flour and leave in a warm place for 1–1½ hours, or until doubled in size.

3 Meanwhile, preheat the oven to 190°C/375°F/ Gas Mark 5. Bake in the preheated oven for 30–35 minutes, or until the crust is a rich brown colour and the base of the loaf sounds hollow when tapped with your knuckles. Transfer to a wire rack to cool.

BANANA & CRANBERRY LOAF

Makes: 1 loaf

Prep: 25 mins,
plus cooling & setting

Cook: 1 hour

Ingredients

butter, for greasing

215 g/7½ oz self-raising flour

½ tsp baking powder

125 g/4½ oz soft
brown sugar

2 bananas, mashed

55 g/2 oz chopped
mixed peel

85 g/3 oz chopped
mixed nuts

40 g/1½ oz dried
cranberries

5–6 tbsp orange juice

2 eggs, lightly beaten

150 ml/5 fl oz vegetable oil

85 g/3 oz icing sugar

grated rind of 1 orange

Method

1 Preheat the oven to 180°C/350°F/Gas Mark 4.
   Grease a 900-g/2-lb loaf tin with butter and line
   the base with baking parchment.

2 Sift the flour and baking powder together into
   a bowl and stir in the sugar, bananas, mixed
   peel, nuts and cranberries. Mix the orange juice,
   eggs and oil together in another bowl, then add
   to the dry ingredients. Stir well with a wooden
   spoon until thoroughly combined.

3 Spoon the mixture into the prepared loaf tin and
   smooth the top. Bake for 1 hour, until golden and
   firm and a cocktail stick inserted into the centre
   of the loaf comes out clean. Turn out on to a wire
   rack to cool.

4 Mix the icing sugar with a little water in a bowl
   and drizzle it over the cooled loaf. Sprinkle the
   orange rind on top and leave to set.

BREADS & SWEET PIES

SOURDOUGH BREAD

Makes: 2 loaves

Prep: 50 mins, plus starter (standing 4–5 days), rising & cooling

Cook: 30 mins

Ingredients

450 g/1 lb wholemeal flour

4 tsp salt

350 ml/12 fl oz lukewarm water

2 tbsp black treacle

1 tbsp vegetable oil, plus extra for brushing

plain flour, for dusting

Starter

85 g/3 oz wholemeal flour

85 g/3 oz strong white flour

55 g/2 oz caster sugar

250 ml/9 fl oz milk

Method

1 For the starter, put the wholemeal flour, strong white flour, sugar and milk into a non-metallic bowl and beat well with a fork. Cover with a damp tea towel and leave to stand at room temperature for 4–5 days, until the mixture is frothy and smells sour.

2 Sift the flour and half the salt together into a bowl and add the water, treacle, oil and starter. Mix well with a wooden spoon until a dough begins to form, then knead with your hands until it leaves the side of the bowl. Turn out onto a lightly floured surface and knead for 10 minutes, or until smooth and elastic.

3 Brush a bowl with oil. Form the dough into a ball, put it into the bowl and put the bowl into a polythene bag or cover with a damp tea towel. Leave to rise in a warm place for 2 hours, or until the dough has doubled in volume.

4 Dust two baking sheets with flour. Mix the remaining salt with 4 tablespoons of water in a bowl. Turn out the dough onto a lightly floured work surface and knock back with your fist, then knead for a further 10 minutes. Halve the dough, shape each piece into an oval and place the loaves on the prepared baking sheets. Brush with

the saltwater glaze and leave to stand in a warm place, brushing frequently with the glaze, for 30 minutes.

5 Preheat the oven to 220°C/425°F/Gas Mark 7. Brush the loaves with the remaining glaze and bake for 30 minutes, or until the crust is golden brown and the loaves sound hollow when tapped on their bases with your knuckles. If it is necessary to bake them for longer, reduce the oven temperature to 190°C/375°F/Gas Mark 5. Transfer to wire racks to cool.

ORANGE MARMALADE LOAF

Makes: 1 loaf

Prep: 40 mins,
plus rising & cooling

Cook: 25–30 mins

Ingredients

450 g/1 lb strong white
bread flour, plus extra
for dusting

1½ tsp salt

1½ tsp caster sugar

1½ tsp easy-blend
dried yeast

150 ml/5 fl oz lukewarm
water

150 ml/5 fl oz lukewarm milk

2 tbsp vegetable oil,
plus extra for brushing

7 tbsp orange marmalade

Topping

1 egg yolk

1 tbsp milk

1 tbsp caster sugar

1–2 tbsp crystallized
orange peel

Method

1 Sift the flour and salt together into a bowl and stir in the sugar and yeast. Make a well in the centre and pour in the lukewarm water, milk and vegetable oil. Stir well with a wooden spoon until the dough begins to come together, then knead with your hands until it leaves the side of the bowl. Turn out on to a lightly floured surface and knead well for about 10 minutes, until smooth and elastic. Brush a bowl with oil. Shape the dough into a ball, place it in the bowl and put the bowl into a plastic bag or cover with a damp tea towel. Leave to rise in a warm place for 1 hour, or until the dough has doubled in volume.

2 Brush a 19 x 12 x 9-cm/7½ x 4½ x 3½-inch loaf tin with oil. Turn out the dough on to a lightly floured surface and knock back with your fist. Roll out to a rectangle about 2 cm/¾-inch thick. Spread the marmalade evenly over the dough leaving a 1-cm/½-inch border along one long side. Roll up the dough like a Swiss roll and put it into the prepared tin, seam side down. Put the tin into a plastic bag or cover with a damp tea towel and leave to rise in a warm place for 45 minutes.

3 Preheat the oven to 220°C/425°F/Gas Mark 7. To make the topping, beat the egg yolk with the milk and sugar in a bowl and brush it over the top of the loaf. Score the top and sprinkle with the orange peel. Bake for 25–30 minutes, until golden brown. Transfer to a wire rack to cool.

APPLE PIE

Serves: 6

Prep: 45 mins,
plus chilling

Cook: 50 mins

Ingredients

Pastry

350 g/12 oz plain flour,
plus extra for dusting

pinch of salt

85 g/3 oz butter or
margarine, diced

85 g/3 oz lard or white
vegetable fat, diced

6 tbsp cold water

beaten egg or milk,
for glazing

Filling

750 g–1 kg/1 lb 10 oz–
2 lb 4 oz cooking apples,
peeled, cored and sliced

125 g/4½ oz caster sugar,
plus extra for sprinkling

½–1 tsp ground cinnamon,
mixed spice or ground
ginger

Method

1 To make the pastry, sift the flour and salt into a
mixing bowl. Add the butter and lard and rub in
with your fingertips until the mixture resembles
fine breadcrumbs. Add the water and gather the
mixture together into a dough. Wrap the dough
in clingfilm and chill in the refrigerator for 30
minutes. Preheat the oven to 220°C/425°F/Gas
Mark 7. Roll out almost two thirds of the pastry
thinly on a lightly floured surface and use to line
a deep 23-cm/9-inch pie dish.

2 To make the filling, place the apple slices, sugar
and spice in a bowl and mix together thoroughly.
Pack the apple mixture into the pastry case;
the filling can come up above the rim. Add
1–2 tablespoons of water if needed.

3 Roll out the remaining pastry on a lightly floured
surface to form a lid. Dampen the edges of the
pie dish with water and position the lid, pressing
the edges firmly together. Trim and crimp the
edges. Use the trimmings to cut out decorations.
Dampen and attach. Glaze the top of the pie
with beaten egg, make 1–2 slits in the top and
place the pie dish on a baking sheet. Bake
in the oven for 20 minutes, then reduce the
temperature to 180°C/350°F/Gas Mark 4 and
bake for a further 30 minutes, or until the pastry
is a golden brown. Serve hot or cold.

BAGELS

Makes: 10

Prep: 45 mins, plus rising, resting & cooling

Cook: 35–40 mins

Ingredients

350 g/12 oz strong white bread flour, plus extra for dusting

2 tsp salt

7 g/¼ oz easy-blend dried yeast

1 tbsp lightly beaten egg

200 ml/7 fl oz lukewarm water

vegetable oil, for brushing

1 egg white

2 tsp water

2 tbsp caraway seeds

Method

1 Sift the flour and salt together into a bowl and stir in the yeast. Make a well in the centre, pour in the egg and lukewarm water and mix to a dough. Turn out on to a lightly floured surface and knead well for about 10 minutes, until smooth.

2 Brush a bowl with vegetable oil. Shape the dough into a ball, place it in the bowl and put the bowl into a plastic bag or cover with a damp tea towel. Leave to rise in a warm place for 1 hour, or until the dough has doubled in volume.

3 Brush 2 baking sheets with oil and dust a tray with flour. Turn out the dough on to a lightly floured surface and knock back with your fist. Knead for 2 minutes, then divide into 10 pieces. Shape each piece into a ball and leave to rest for 5 minutes. Gently flatten each ball with a lightly floured hand and make a hole in the centre with the handle of a wooden spoon. Put the bagels on the floured tray, put the tray in a plastic bag or cover with a damp tea towel and leave to rise in a warm place for 20 minutes.

4 Meanwhile, preheat the oven to 220°C/425°F/ Gas Mark 7 and bring a large pan of water to the boil. Lower the heat until the water is barely simmering, then add 2 bagels. Poach for

1 minute, then turn over and poach for a further 30 seconds. Remove with a slotted spoon and drain on a tea towel. Poach the remaining bagels in the same way.

5 Transfer the bagels to the prepared baking sheets. Beat the egg white with the water in a bowl and brush it over the bagels. Sprinkle with the caraway seeds and bake for 25–30 minutes, until golden brown. Transfer to a wire rack to cool.

CROWN LOAF

Serves: 9

Prep: 40 mins, plus rising, cooling & setting

Cook: 20–30 mins

Ingredients

225 g/8 oz strong white flour

½ tsp salt

7 g/¼ oz easy-blend dried yeast

2 tbsp butter, diced, plus extra for greasing

125 ml/4 fl oz lukewarm milk

1 egg, lightly beaten

Filling

4 tbsp butter, softened

50 g/1¾ oz soft light brown sugar

2 tbsp chopped hazelnuts

1 tbsp crystallized ginger

50 g/1¾ oz chopped mixed peel

1 tbsp dark rum or brandy

Icing

115 g/4 oz icing sugar, sifted

1–2 tbsp lemon juice

Method

1 Grease a baking tray. Sift the flour and salt into a bowl. Stir in the yeast. Rub in the diced butter with your fingertips. Add the milk and egg and mix to form a dough. Place the dough in a greased bowl, cover and leave in a warm place for 40 minutes, or until doubled in volume.

2 Punch down lightly for 1 minute. Roll out to a 30 x 23-cm/12 x 9-inch rectangle. For the filling, cream the butter and sugar until light and fluffy. Stir in the hazelnuts, ginger, mixed peel and rum. Spread the filling over the dough, leaving a 2.5-cm/1-inch border.

3 Roll up the dough, starting from one of the long edges, into a sausage shape. Cut into slices at 5-cm/2-inch intervals and place in a circle on the prepared baking tray with the slices just touching.

4 Cover and leave in a warm place for 30 minutes. Meanwhile, preheat the oven to 190°C/375°F/ Gas Mark 5. Bake the loaf in the oven for 20–30 minutes, or until golden.

5 For the icing, mix the sugar with enough lemon juice to form a thin icing. Leave the loaf to cool slightly before drizzling with the icing. Allow the icing to set before serving.

BREADS & SWEET PIES

DEEP SOUTH CHERRY PIES

Makes: 24

Prep: 45 mins,
plus cooling

Cook: 15 mins

Ingredients

butter, for greasing

350 g/12 oz cherries, stoned
and halved, plus extra
to decorate

2 tsp cornflour

3 tbsp caster sugar

1 tsp vanilla extract

½ tsp ground cinnamon

450 g/1 lb ready-made
sweet shortcrust pastry,
chilled

plain flour, for dusting

1 egg yolk mixed with
1 tbsp water, to glaze

2 tbsp caster sugar mixed
with a large pinch ground
cinnamon, for sprinkling

Method

1 Preheat the oven to 180°C/350°F/Gas Mark 4.
Lightly grease two x 12-section mini muffin tins.
Put the stoned cherries in a mixing bowl and
stir in the cornflour, sugar, vanilla extract
and cinnamon.

2 Roll two-thirds of the pastry out thinly on a lightly
floured surface. Using a fluted cookie cutter,
stamp out 24 circles, each 6 cm/2½ inches
in diameter. Press these into the prepared tins,
rerolling the trimmings as needed. Brush the top
edges of the pie cases with a little of the egg
glaze, then spoon in the filling.

3 Roll the reserved pastry out thinly on a lightly
floured surface. Stamp out 24 circles, each
5 cm/2 inches in diameter, rerolling the trimmings
as needed. Arrange these on top of the pies,
pressing the edges together to seal. Use a cookie
cutter to cut tiny hearts and flowers from the
remaining pastry and arrange these on the lids.
Brush over the decorated lids with egg glaze.

4 Bake in the preheated oven for 15 minutes,
or until golden. Leave to cool in the tins for 10
minutes, then loosen with a round-bladed knife
and transfer to a wire rack to cool. Serve warm
or cold, sprinkled with the cinnamon sugar, on a
plate decorated with extra cherries.

BREADS & SWEET PIES

PISTACHIO & ALMOND TARTS

Makes: 12

Prep: 30 mins,
plus cooling

Cook: 15 mins

Ingredients

225 g/8 oz ready-made sweet shortcrust pastry, chilled

plain flour, for dusting

50 g/1¾ oz butter, softened, plus extra for greasing

50 g/1¾ oz caster sugar

1 egg yolk

50 g/1¾ oz ground almonds

a few drops of almond extract or orange flower water

1½ tbsp flaked almonds

1 tbsp pistachio nuts, thinly sliced

icing sugar, sifted, to decorate

Method

1 Lightly grease a 12-section mini muffin tin. Preheat the oven to 180°C/350°F/Gas Mark 4.

2 Roll the pastry out thinly on a lightly floured surface. Using a fluted cookie cutter, stamp out 12 circles each 6 cm/2½ inches in diameter. Press these gently into the prepared tin, rerolling the trimmings as needed.

3 Put the butter and caster sugar in a mixing bowl and beat together until light and fluffy. Beat in the egg yolk, then the ground almonds. Flavour with a little almond essence.

4 Spoon the filling into the pastry cases.

5 Sprinkle the flaked almonds and sliced pistachios over the top and press them lightly into the filling.

6 Bake in the preheated oven for 15 minutes, or until the almonds are golden. Leave to cool in the tin for 10 minutes, then loosen with a round-bladed knife and transfer to a wire rack to cool. Serve warm or cold, dusted with sifted icing sugar.

CHOCOLATE CRUMBLE PIE

Serves: 8

Prep: 40 mins,
plus chilling & resting

Cook: 35 mins

Ingredients

175 g/6 oz plain flour
1 tsp baking powder
115 g/4 oz unsalted butter,
diced
55 g/2 oz caster sugar
1 egg yolk
1–2 tsp cold water

Filling

150 ml/5 fl oz double cream
150 ml/5 fl oz milk
225 g/8 oz plain chocolate,
chopped
2 eggs, beaten

Crumble topping

115 g/4 oz soft light
brown sugar
85 g/3 oz toasted
pecan nuts
115 g/4 oz plain chocolate
85 g/3 oz amaretti biscuits
1 tsp cocoa powder

Method

1 To make the pastry, sift the flour and baking powder into a large bowl. Rub in the butter and stir in the caster sugar, then add the egg yolk and the water to bring the dough together. Turn the dough out and knead briefly. Wrap the dough and chill in the refrigerator for 30 minutes. Meanwhile, preheat the oven to 190°C/375°F/ Gas Mark 5.

2 Roll out the pastry and use it to line a 23-cm/ 9-inch loose-based fluted tart tin. Prick the base with a fork. Line with baking paper, fill with baking beans and bake in the preheated oven for 15 minutes. Remove the paper and beans. Reduce the oven temperature to 180°C/350°F/ Gas Mark 4.

3 For the filling, bring the cream and milk to the boil in a saucepan, remove from the heat and add the chocolate. Stir until melted and smooth. Add the eggs, mix well and pour into the pastry case. Bake for 15 minutes, remove from the oven and leave to rest for 1 hour.

4 When you are ready to serve the pie, put the brown sugar in a large bowl. Chop the nuts and chocolate with a large knife and crush the biscuits, then add to the bowl with the cocoa and mix well. Sprinkle over the pie.

BREADS & SWEET PIES

CHOCOLATE PEANUT BUTTER PIE

Serves: 8

Prep: 15 mins, plus cooling & chilling

Cook: 20 mins

Ingredients

Biscuit crust

225 g/8 oz bourbon biscuits, finely crushed

25 g/1 oz plain chocolate, grated

70 g/2½ oz butter, melted

Filling

175 g/6 oz cream cheese

140 g/5 oz smooth peanut butter

25 g/1 oz caster sugar

200 ml/7 fl oz double cream

Chocolate glaze

115 g/4 oz plain chocolate, broken into pieces

1 tbsp golden syrup

25 g/1 oz unsalted butter

100 ml/3½ fl oz double cream

chopped roasted peanuts, to decorate

Method

1 Preheat the oven to 180°C/350°F/Gas Mark 4. Put the biscuit crumbs into a bowl and stir in the grated chocolate and melted butter. Press the mixture into the base and up the sides of a 23-cm/9-inch tart tin. Bake in the preheated oven for 10 minutes, or until just set. Leave to cool.

2 To make the filling, put the cream cheese and peanut butter into a bowl and beat together until smooth. Beat in the sugar, then gradually beat in the cream. Spoon the mixture into the biscuit case and gently level the surface. Chill in the refrigerator for 30 minutes.

3 To make the glaze, put the chocolate, syrup and butter into a heatproof bowl set over a saucepan of simmering water and heat until melted. Remove from the heat and stir in the cream until smooth. Leave to cool for 10–20 minutes, or until thickened, then gently spread over the filling. Chill in the refrigerator for at least 1 hour before serving.

4 To serve, remove the pie from the tin and decorate with chopped roasted peanuts.

★ Variation

To make extra delicious, decorate with some dark chocolate sauce and some raspberries.

PUMPKIN PIE

Serves: 8

Prep: 25 mins,
plus cooling & chilling

**Cook: 50 mins-
1 hour**

Ingredients

plain flour, for dusting

350 g/12 oz ready-made
shortcrust pastry

400 g/14 oz pumpkin purée

2 eggs, lightly beaten

150 g/5½ oz white sugar

1 tsp ground cinnamon

½ tsp ground ginger

¼ tsp ground cloves

½ tsp salt

350 ml/12 fl oz canned
evaporated milk

Eggnog whipped cream

350 ml/12 fl oz double
cream

70 g/2½ oz icing sugar

1 tbsp brandy, or to taste

1 tbsp light or dark rum,
or to taste

freshly grated nutmeg,
to decorate

Method

1 Preheat the oven to 200°C/400°F/Gas Mark 6.
Very lightly dust a rolling pin with flour and use
to roll out the pastry on a lightly floured work
surface into a 30-cm/12-inch round. Line a
23-cm/9-inch deep pie dish with the pastry,
trimming the excess. Line the pastry case with
baking paper and fill with dried beans. Bake in
the oven for 10 minutes. Remove from the oven
and take out the paper and beans. Reduce the
oven temperature to 180°C/350°F/Gas Mark 4.

2 Meanwhile, put the pumpkin purée, eggs, sugar,
cinnamon, ginger, cloves and salt into a bowl
and beat together, then beat in the evaporated
milk. Pour the mixture into the pastry case, return
to the oven, and bake for 40–50 minutes until
the filling is set and a knife inserted in the centre
comes out clean. Transfer to a wire rack to cool.

3 While the pie is baking, make the eggnog
whipped cream. Put the cream in a bowl and
beat until it has thickened and increased in
volume. Just as it starts to stiffen, sift over the
icing sugar and continue beating until it holds
stiff peaks. Add the brandy and rum and beat,
taking care not to overbeat or the mixture will
separate. Cover and chill until required. To serve,
grate some nutmeg over the whipped cream.
Serve with the cream.

BANOFFEE PIE

Serves: 10

Prep: 30 mins, plus cooling

Cook: 2 ¼–2 ½ hours

Ingredients

Filling

3 x 400 g/14 oz canned sweetened condensed milk

4 ripe bananas

juice of ½ lemon

1 tsp vanilla extract

75 g/2¾ oz plain chocolate, grated

475 ml/17 fl oz double cream, whipped

Biscuit crust

85 g/3 oz butter, melted, plus extra for greasing

150 g/5½ oz digestive biscuits, finely crushed

25 g/1 oz almonds, toasted and ground

25 g/1 oz hazelnuts, toasted and ground

Method

1 Place the unopened cans of condensed milk in a large saucepan and add enough water to cover them. Bring to the boil, then reduce the heat and simmer for 2 hours, topping up the water level to keep the cans covered. Carefully lift out the hot cans from the pan and leave to cool.

2 Preheat the oven to 180°C/350°F/Gas Mark 4. To make the crust, place the butter in a bowl and add the crushed digestive biscuits and ground nuts. Mix together well, then press the mixture evenly into the base and sides of a greased 23-cm/9-inch tart tin. Bake in the preheated oven for 10–12 minutes. Leave to cool.

3 Peel and slice the bananas and place in a bowl. Squeeze over the juice from the lemon, add the vanilla extract and mix together. Spread the banana mixture over the biscuit crust in the tin, then spoon over the contents of the cooled cans of condensed milk.

4 Sprinkle over 50 g/1¾ oz of the chocolate, then top with a layer of whipped cream. Sprinkle over the remaining grated chocolate and serve the pie at room temperature.

PEACH CRUMB PIE

Serves: 6

Prep: 45 mins,
plus chilling

Cook: 40–45 mins

Ingredients

Pastry

200 g/7 oz plain flour,
plus extra for dusting

100 g/3½ oz butter, diced

1 egg yolk

1 tsp lemon juice

1–2 tbsp iced water

Crumb topping

115 g/4 oz self-raising flour

70 g/2½ oz butter, diced

55 g/2 oz demerara sugar

Filling

600 g/1 lb 5 oz just ripe
peaches, halved, stoned
and sliced

25 g/1 oz caster sugar

1 tbsp cornflour

Method

1 To make the pastry, sift the flour into a bowl and add the butter. Rub the butter into the flour until it resembles fine breadcrumbs. Mix together the egg yolk and lemon juice with 1 tablespoon of the water. Stir into the flour mixture and mix to a firm dough, adding more water if necessary. Knead lightly until smooth. Wrap in clingfilm and chill in the refrigerator for 30 minutes.

2 Roll out the pastry on a lightly floured work surface and use to line a 23-cm/9-inch pie dish or loose-based round tart tin. Prick the base all over with a fork. Chill in the refrigerator for 15 minutes. Preheat the oven to 200°C/400°F/ Gas Mark 6 and preheat a baking sheet. Line the pastry case with baking paper and baking beans. Place on the heated baking sheet and bake for 10 minutes. Remove the paper and beans and bake for a further 5–6 minutes, or until the pastry is light golden. Reduce the oven temperature to 190°C/375°F/Gas Mark 5.

3 To make the crumb topping, place the flour and butter in a bowl and rub in the butter until crumbly. Stir in the sugar. To make the filling, place the peach slices in a bowl with the sugar and cornflour and toss well to mix. Transfer to the pastry case, then sprinkle over the crumb topping. Bake in the oven for 25–30 minutes, or until the topping is golden. Serve warm or cold.

PEACH & CHOCOLATE MERINGUE PIES

Makes: 6

Prep: 45 mins,
plus chilling & cooling

Cook: 20–25 mins

Ingredients

225 g/8 oz ready-made
sweet shortcrust pastry,
chilled

plain flour, for dusting

25 g/1 oz butter,
plus extra for greasing

2 peaches, peeled if liked,
halved, stoned and diced

50 g/1¾ oz dark chocolate,
roughly chopped

2 egg whites

55 g/2 oz caster sugar

Method

1 Lightly grease a 6-section muffin tin. Roll the pastry out thinly on a lightly floured surface. Using a plain cookie cutter, stamp out 6 circles each 10 cm/4 inches in diameter. Press these gently into the prepared tin, rerolling the trimmings as needed. Prick the base of each pie with a fork, then chill in the fridge for 15 minutes. Preheat the oven to 190°C/375°F/Gas Mark 5.

2 Line the pastry cases with squares of crumpled baking paper and baking beans. Bake in the preheated oven for 10 minutes. Remove the paper and beans and cook the pastry cases for 2–3 minutes more, or until the base of the pastry is crisp and dry.

3 Meanwhile, melt the butter in a small frying pan or saucepan, add the peaches and cook gently for 5 minutes, stirring occasionally, until softened. Spoon the peaches into the pastry cases.

4 Put the chocolate in a heatproof bowl, set over a saucepan of gently simmering water and heat until melted. Whisk the egg whites in a large clean mixing bowl until you have stiff, moist-looking peaks, then gradually whisk in the sugar a teaspoon at a time for another 1–2 minutes, or until the meringue is very thick and glossy. Fold

the melted chocolate into the meringue with just a couple of swirls of the spoon for a marbled effect. Spoon into the pies.

5 Bake in the preheated oven for 5–7 minutes, or until the meringue peaks are golden and just cooked through. Leave to cool in the tin for 10 minutes, then loosen with a round-bladed knife and transfer to a wire rack to cool. Serve warm.

BOSTON CREAM PIE

Serves: 8

Prep: 35 mins,
plus chilling & cooling

Cook: 35 mins

Ingredients

225 g/8 oz self-raising flour

½ tsp salt

1 tsp baking powder

115 g/4 oz unsalted butter, softened, plus extra for greasing

200 g/7 oz caster sugar

2 eggs, beaten

175 ml/6 fl oz milk

Pastry cream

100 g/3½ oz caster sugar

2 tbsp cornflour

3 eggs

225 ml/8 fl oz double cream

225 ml/8 fl oz milk

15 g/½ oz unsalted butter

1½ tsp vanilla extract

pinch of salt

Chocolate topping

115 g/4 oz plain chocolate, broken into pieces

125 ml/4 fl oz double cream

1 tsp butter

Method

1. To make the pastry cream, whisk together the sugar, cornflour and eggs until the whisk leaves a ribbon trail when lifted. Set aside. Bring the cream, milk and butter to the boil in a pan. Add the sugar mixture and boil, whisking constantly, for 1 minute, until thickened, then strain into a bowl. Cover the surface with clingfilm and chill overnight.

2. Preheat the oven to 190°C/375°F/Gas Mark 5. Grease two 20-cm/8-inch sandwich tins. Sift the flour, salt and baking powder into a bowl and set aside. Cream together the butter and sugar until pale and fluffy. Gradually add the eggs, mixing well after each addition. Gradually add the milk, alternating with the flour mixture, and stir to combine. Divide the mixture between the prepared tins. Bake in the preheated oven for 25 minutes, until well risen and firm to the touch. Turn out onto a wire rack to cool.

3. Put the chocolate into a heatproof bowl. Bring the cream and butter to simmering point in a small saucepan, then pour over the chocolate. Leave to stand for 3 minutes, then whisk gently to mix. Leave to cool and thicken. Whisk the vanilla extract and salt into the pastry cream, then spread it over one of the cakes. Top with the second cake, then spread with the chocolate topping.

COFFEE TARTS

Makes: 12

Prep: 45 mins,
plus chilling & cooling

Cook: 30–35 mins

Ingredients

butter, for greasing

450 g/1 lb ready-made
sweet shortcrust pastry,
chilled

a little plain flour, for dusting

225 ml/8 fl oz semi-skimmed
milk

115 g/4 oz plain chocolate,
roughly chopped

2 tsp instant coffee powder
or granules

2 tbsp caster sugar

2 eggs

2 egg yolks

Decoration

200 ml/7 fl oz double cream

2 tbsp icing sugar

2 tbsp coffee cream liqueur

1½ tsp instant coffee
dissolved in 1 tsp
boiling water

white chocolate curls,
to decorate

a dusting of cocoa, sifted,
to decorate

Method

1 Lightly grease a 12-section muffin tin. Roll the pastry out thinly on a lightly floured surface. Using a plain cookie cutter, stamp out 12 circles each 10 cm/4 inches in diameter. Press these gently into the prepared tin. Prick the base of each with a fork, then chill for 15 minutes. Preheat the oven to 190°C/375°F/Gas Mark 5.

2 Line the pastry cases with squares of crumpled baking paper and baking beans. Bake for 10 minutes. Remove the paper and beans and cook the cases for 2–3 minutes more, or until the base of the pastry is crisp. Turn the oven down to 160°C/325°F/Gas Mark 3. Meanwhile, bring the milk just to the boil in a small saucepan. Add the chocolate, coffee and caster sugar and leave to stand, off the heat, until the chocolate has melted.

3 Beat the eggs and yolks in a mixing bowl, then gradually whisk in the warm milk mixture until smooth. Pour the custard into the pastry cases.

4 Bake in the preheated oven for 15–20 minutes, or until just set. Leave to cool in the tin for 10 minutes, then loosen with a round-bladed knife and transfer to a wire rack. Whip the cream in a bowl until it forms soft swirls. Add the sugar, then whisk in the liqueur and coffee until thick. Spoon over the pies, then decorate with white chocolate curls and a dusting of cocoa.

BREADS & SWEET PIES

COCONUT CREAM PIE

Serves: 6

Prep: 30 mins,
plus chilling & cooling

Cook: 25–30 mins

Ingredients

250 g/9 oz ready-made
shortcrust pastry, thawed,
if frozen

2 eggs

55 g/2 oz caster sugar

1 tsp vanilla extract

2 tbsp plain flour,
plus extra for dusting

2 tbsp cornflour

150 ml/5 fl oz milk

200 ml/7 fl oz coconut milk

25 g/1 oz desiccated
coconut

400 ml/14 fl oz double
cream

2 tbsp toasted desiccated
coconut, to decorate

Method

1 Preheat the oven to 200°C/400°F/Gas Mark 6.
Roll the pastry out on a lightly floured surface
and use to line a 20–23-cm/8–9-inch pie dish. Trim
and crimp the edges. Prick the base with a fork
and chill in the refrigerator for 15 minutes.

2 Line the pastry case with baking paper and
baking beans. Bake blind in the preheated
oven for 10 minutes. Remove the paper and
beans and bake for a further 6–8 minutes,
or until golden. Leave to cool.

3 For the filling, whisk together the eggs, sugar
and vanilla extract in a bowl. Blend the flour
and cornflour to a paste with 4 tablespoons of
milk, then whisk the paste into the egg mixture.
Heat the remaining milk and coconut milk in a
saucepan until almost boiling and pour onto
the egg mixture, stirring constantly. Return to
the saucepan and slowly heat, whisking until
smooth and thick. Stir in the coconut. Cover
with dampened greaseproof paper and leave
until cold.

4 Spread the coconut filling in the pastry case.
Whip the cream until holding soft peaks and
spread over the top of the filling. Sprinkle over
the toasted coconut and serve.

BREADS & SWEET PIES

MAPLE & PECAN PIE

Serves: 8

Prep: 30 mins, plus chilling & cooling

Cook: 55 mins– 1 hour

Ingredients

Pastry

175 g/6 oz plain flour, plus extra for dusting

85 g/3 oz butter, diced

1 tbsp caster sugar

1 egg, beaten with 1 tbsp cold water

Filling

85 g/3 oz butter

85 g/3 oz soft light brown sugar

150 ml/5 fl oz maple syrup

5 tbsp golden syrup

3 large eggs, beaten

1 tsp vanilla extract

200 g/7 oz pecan nuts

Method

1 To make the pastry, sift the flour into a bowl and add the butter. Rub the butter into the flour until the mixture resembles fine breadcrumbs. Stir in the caster sugar and egg and water mixture and mix to a firm dough.

2 Turn out the dough onto a lightly floured work surface and lightly knead until smooth. Roll out and use to line a 24-cm/9½-inch loose-based tart tin. Prick the dough all over with a fork and chill in the refrigerator for 30 minutes. Meanwhile, preheat the oven to 200°C/400°F/Gas Mark 6.

3 Place the tin on a baking sheet and line with baking paper and baking beans. Bake blind in the preheated oven for 10 minutes, then remove the paper and beans and bake for a further 5 minutes, or until the pastry is light golden. Reduce the oven temperature to 180°C/350°F/Gas Mark 4. To make the filling, place the butter, brown sugar, maple syrup and golden syrup in a saucepan and heat over a low heat until melted. Leave to cool for 5 minutes, then beat in the eggs and vanilla extract. Chop half of the pecan nuts and stir into the mixture.

4 Pour the mixture into the pastry case and scatter over the remaining nuts. Bake in the preheated oven for 35–45 minutes, or until the filling is just set. Serve warm or cold.

BREADS & SWEET PIES

LEMON & BLUEBERRY CHEESE PIES

Makes: 12

Prep: 45 mins,
plus cooling & chilling

Cook: 40–45 mins

Ingredients

2 tbsp golden syrup

100 g/3½ oz butter, plus extra for greasing

300 g/10½ oz milk chocolate digestives, crushed

400 g/14 oz full-fat cream cheese

150 g/5½ oz caster sugar

150 ml/5 fl oz double cream

2 eggs

grated rind and juice of 1 lemon

400 g/14 oz blueberries

2 tsp cornflour

4 tbsp water

250 ml/9 fl oz crème fraîche, to serve

Method

1 Preheat the oven to 180°C/350°F/Gas Mark 4. Lightly grease a 12-section muffin tin.

2 Put the syrup and butter in a small saucepan. Heat gently, uncovered, stirring, until the butter has just melted. Take the saucepan off the heat and stir in the biscuit crumbs. Divide the mixture between the sections of the prepared tin. Press it firmly over the base and sides of the tin using the back of a teaspoon.

3 Line the cases with baking paper and baking beans, then bake them in the preheated oven for 8–10 minutes, or until slightly darker in colour. Leave to cool and harden in the tin for 10–15 minutes. Remove the paper and beans. Turn the oven down to 150°C/300°F/Gas Mark 2.

4 Put the cream cheese into a mixing bowl. Add 115 g/4 oz of the sugar and beat together briefly with an electric handheld whisk. Gradually beat in the cream and then the eggs until smooth. Add the lemon rind, then stir in half the juice. Spoon the filling into the crumb cases.

5 Bake in the preheated oven for 15–20 minutes, or until the filling is just set with a slight wobble to the centre. Turn the oven off, open the door slightly and leave the pies to cool in the oven.

6 For the topping, put half the blueberries in a medium saucepan. Add the cornflour, remaining sugar and remaining lemon juice, then stir in the water. Cook over a low heat until the juice begins to run from the blueberries, then increase the heat and cook until the sauce has thickened. Add the remaining blueberries and cook for 2 minutes more. Take off the heat and leave to cool.

7 Loosen the pies with a round-bladed knife and transfer to a plate. Chill in the fridge for several hours. When ready to serve, top each with a spoonful of crème fraîche and a generous spoonful of the blueberries.

LEMON MERINGUE PIE

Serves: 8

Prep: 40 mins,
plus chilling & cooling

Cook: 1 hour

Ingredients

Pastry

150 g/5½ oz plain flour, plus extra for dusting

85 g/3 oz butter, diced, plus extra for greasing

35 g/1¼ oz icing sugar, sifted

finely grated rind of ½ lemon

½ egg yolk, beaten

1½ tbsp milk

Filling

3 tbsp cornflour

300 ml/10 fl oz water

juice and grated rind of 2 lemons

175 g/6 oz caster sugar

2 eggs, separated

Method

1 To make the pastry, sift the flour into a bowl. Rub in the butter until the mixture resembles fine breadcrumbs. Mix in the remaining pastry ingredients. Turn out onto a lightly floured work surface and knead briefly. Wrap in clingfilm and chill in the refrigerator for 30 minutes.

2 Preheat the oven to 180°C/350°F/Gas Mark 4. Grease a 20-cm/8-inch tart tin. Roll out the pastry to a thickness of 5 mm/¼ inch on a lightly floured surface, then use it to line the base and sides of the tin. Prick all over with a fork, line with baking paper and fill with baking beans. Bake blind in the oven for 15 minutes. Remove the pastry case from the oven and take out the paper and beans. Reduce the oven temperature to 150°C/300°F/Gas Mark 2.

3 To make the filling, mix the cornflour with a little of the water to form a paste. Put the remaining water in a saucepan. Stir in the lemon juice, lemon rind and cornflour paste. Bring to the boil, stirring. Cook for 2 minutes. Leave to cool slightly. Stir in 5 tablespoons of the caster sugar and the egg yolks, then pour into the pastry case. Whisk the egg whites until they hold stiff peaks. Gradually whisk in the remaining caster sugar and spread over the pie. Bake for a further 40 minutes. Remove from the oven, cool and serve.

KEY LIME PIE

Serves: 8

Prep: 30 mins,
plus cooling & chilling

Cook: 20–25 mins

Ingredients

Crumb crust

175 g/6 oz digestive or
ginger biscuits

2 tbsp caster sugar

½ tsp ground cinnamon

70 g/2½ oz butter, melted,
plus extra for greasing

Filling

400 ml/14 fl oz canned
condensed milk

125 ml/4 fl oz freshly
squeezed lime juice

finely grated rind of 3 limes

4 egg yolks

whipped cream, to serve

Method

1 Preheat the oven to 160°C/325°F/Gas Mark 3.
Lightly grease a 23-cm/9-inch tart tin, about
4 cm/1½ inch deep. To make the crumb crust,
put the biscuits, sugar and cinnamon in a food
processor and process until fine crumbs form –
do not overprocess to a powder. Add the melted
butter and process again until moistened.

2 Tip the crumb mixture into the prepared tart tin
and press over the base and up the sides. Place
the tart tin on a baking sheet and bake in the
preheated oven for 5 minutes. Meanwhile, to
make the filling, beat the condensed milk, lime
juice, lime rind and egg yolks together in a bowl
until well blended.

3 Remove the tart tin from the oven, pour the
filling into the crumb crust and spread out to
the edges. Return to the oven for a further
15 minutes, or until the filling is set around the
edges but still wobbly in the centre. Leave to
cool completely on a wire rack, then cover and
chill for at least 2 hours. Spread with whipped
cream and serve.

★ **Variation**

Instead of cream, top the pie with meringue and
brown briefly in a hot oven.

BREADS & SWEET PIES

INDEX

INDEX

This edition published by Parragon Books Ltd in 2014
LOVE FOOD is an imprint of Parragon Books Ltd

Parragon Books Ltd
Chartist House
15–17 Trim Street
Bath BA1 1HA, UK
www.parragon.com/lovefood

ISBN 978-1-4723-5996-4
Printed in China

Cover photography by Ian Garlick
Introduction by Anne Sheasby

Bundt ® is a registered trade mark of Northland Aluminium Products, Inc.

Notes for the Reader
This book uses both metric and imperial measurements. Follow the same units of measurement throughout; do not mix metric and imperial. All spoon measurements are level: teaspoons are assumed to be 5 ml, and tablespoons are assumed to be 15 ml. Unless otherwise stated, milk is assumed to be full fat, eggs and individual vegetables are medium, and pepper is freshly ground black pepper. Unless otherwise stated, all root vegetables should be peeled prior to using.

Garnishes, decorations and serving suggestions are all optional and not necessarily included in the recipe ingredients or method. The times given are an approximate guide only. Preparation times differ according to the techniques used by different people and the cooking times may also vary from those given. Optional ingredients, variations or serving suggestions have not been included in the time calculations.

150 Recipes series

150
BAKING
recipes
INSPIRED IDEAS FOR EVERYDAY COOKING

150
CAKE
recipes
INSPIRED IDEAS FOR EVERYDAY COOKING

150
CHICKEN
recipes
INSPIRED IDEAS FOR EVERYDAY COOKING

150
CUPCAKE
& MUFFIN
recipes
INSPIRED IDEAS FOR EVERYDAY COOKING

150
FAST
& SIMPLE
recipes
INSPIRED IDEAS FOR EVERYDAY COOKING

150
INDIAN
recipes
INSPIRED IDEAS FOR EVERYDAY COOKING

150
PASTA
recipes
INSPIRED IDEAS FOR EVERYDAY COOKING

150
SLOW
COOKER
recipes
INSPIRED IDEAS FOR EVERYDAY COOKING

150
STIR-FRY
recipes
INSPIRED IDEAS FOR EVERYDAY COOKING

150
STUDENT
recipes
INSPIRED IDEAS FOR EVERYDAY COOKING

150
TAPAS
recipes
INSPIRED IDEAS FOR EVERYDAY COOKING

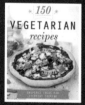

150
VEGETARIAN
recipes
INSPIRED IDEAS FOR EVERYDAY COOKING